Wood Pellet Smoker and Grill Cookbook

Learn to Make 200+ Easy and Mouthwatering Grill Recipes To Make Your Picnics and Gatherings Memorable

NELSON KNIGHT

© **Copyright 2021 by NELSON KNIGHT All rights reserved.**

This document is geared towards providing exact and reliable information in regards to the topic and issue covered. The publication is sold with the idea that the publisher is not required to render accounting, officially permitted, or otherwise, qualified services. If advice is necessary, legal or professional, a practiced individual in the profession should be ordered.

- From a Declaration of Principles which was accepted and approved equally by a Committee of the American Bar Association and a Committee of Publishers and Associations.

In no way is it legal to reproduce, duplicate, or transmit any part of this document in either electronic means or in printed format. Recording of this publication is strictly prohibited and any storage of this document is not allowed unless with written permission from the publisher. All rights reserved.

The information provided herein is stated to be truthful and consistent, in that any liability, in terms of inattention or otherwise, by any usage or abuse of any policies, processes, or directions contained within is the solitary and utter responsibility of the recipient reader. Under no circumstances will any legal responsibility or blame be held against the publisher for any reparation, damages, or monetary loss due to the information herein, either directly or indirectly.

Respective authors own all copyrights not held by the publisher.

The information herein is offered for informational purposes solely, and is universal as so. The presentation of the information is without contract or any type of guarantee assurance. The trademarks that are used are without any consent, and the publication of the trademark is without permission or backing by the trademark owner. All trademarks and brands within this book are for clarifying purposes only and are the owned by the owners themselves, not affiliated with this document.

Contents

Introduction 7

CHAPTER 1: Wood Pellet Smoker & Grill Beef Recipes 9

1.1 Sweet Tea Marinated Ribeyes 9
1.2 Porterhouse with Summer Au Poivre Sauce 11
1.3 Hasselback Short Rib Bulgogi 12
1.4 Grilled Steak Tacos 13
1.5 Brisket 14
1.6 Santa Maria Roast Beef 15
1.7 California Burger Wraps 16
1.8 Grilled Flank Steak 17
1.9 Juicy Grilled Burgers 18
1.10 Jalapeño Popper Burgers 19
1.11 Steak Fajitas 20
1.12 Lacquered Rib Eye 22
1.13 Classic burgers 23
1.14 Pulled Beef Burritos 24
1.15 Garlic and Red-Miso Porterhouse 25
1.16 Top Round Beef Roast Recipe 26
1.17 Brisket Burger 27
1.18 Boneless Rib Eye with Chimichurri 28
1.19 Grilled Cowboy Steak 29
1.20 Florentine Steak 30
1.21 Glazed Flank Steak 31
1.22 Angel Cruz Beef Skewers 32
1.23 Steak Sandwich Kabobs 33
1.24 Tacos on a Stick 34
1.25 Dry Rubbed Smoked Brisket 35
1.26 Beef Suya 36
1.27 Cola Burgers 37
1.28 Grilled Roast Beef Recipe 38
1.30 Tri-Tip Roast 39
1.31 Perfectly Grilled Steak 40

CHAPTER 2: Wood Pellet Smoker & Grill Chicken Recipes 41

2.1 Chicken Caprese Sandwich 41
2.2 Grilled Butterflied Chicken with Lemongrass Sauce 42

2.3 California Grilled Chicken 44
2.4 Sticky Grilled Chicken 45
2.5 Grilled Chicken Breasts with Lemon and Thyme 46
2.6 Peruvian Chicken 47
2.7 Grilled Chicken Shawarma 49
2.8 Bratwurst and Chicken Kabobs 50
2.9 Thai turkey burger 51
2.10 Applewood Smoked Chicken 52
2.11 Smoked Turkey Breast 54
2.12 Sticky Barbecue Chicken 55
2.13 Grilled Teriyaki Chicken Bowl 57
2.14 Chicken Breasts with Romesco Sauce 58
2.15 Grilled Chicken Burgers 60
2.16 Chicken with Salsa Verde 61
2.17 Cuban Mojo Chicken Legs 62
2.18 Juicy Grilled Chicken Breast 64
2.19 Yogurt-Marinated Chicken Thighs 65
2.20 Buttermilk Brined Rotisserie Chicken 66

CHAPTER 3: Wood Pellet Smoker & Grill Lamb Recipes 68

3.1 Grilled Herb Crusted Rack of Lamb 68
3.2 Steakburger with Tangy Caramelized Onions and Herb Butter 69
3.3 Grain Bowls with Grilled Corn, Steak, and Avocado 71
3.4 Racks of Lamb with Roasted-Shallot Vinaigrette 72
3.5 Grilled Lamb Chops 73
3.6 Rosemary Lamb Chops 74
3.7 Fire Roasted Baby Lamb Chops with Smoked Paprika-Orange BBQ Sauce
.... 75
3.8 Lamb Chops Grilled in Rosemary Smoke 76
3.9 Make-Ahead Instant Pot Grilled Ribs 77
3.10 3-Ingredient Grilled Steak, Pineapple, and Avocado Salad .. 78

CHAPTER 4: Wood Pellet Smoker & Grill Seafood Recipes 80

4.1 Grilled Sea Scallops with Corn Salad 80
4.2 Salmon with Grilled Lemons and Yogurt Sauce 81
4.3 Garlic Butter Salmon 83
4.4 Lobster Tails with Basil-Lemon Butter 84
4.5 Grilled Cedar Plank Salmon Burgers 85
4.6 Grilled Shrimp with Shrimp Butter 86

4.7 Grilled Shellfish and Vegetables al Cartoccio 87
4.8 Grilled Shrimp with Oregano and Lemon 88
4.9 Grilled Fish 89
4.10 Cajun Garlic Butter Lobster Tails 89
4.11 Lemony Grilled Salmon 90
4.12 Grilled Halibut 91
4.13 Maple Glazed Salmon Steaks 92

CHAPTER 5: Wood Pellet Smoker & Grill Vegetables & Sides Recipes 94

5.1 Grilled Eggplant Salad with Freekeh and Yogurt Dressing 94
5.2 Mexican-Style Corn on the Cob 96
5.3 Roasted Root Vegetables with Garlic and Rosemary 97
5.4 Spicy Grilled Broccoli 98
5.5 Grilled Carrots 99
5.6 Grilled Pattypans 100
5.7 Grilled Potato Salad with Chiles and Basil 100
5.8 Grilled Artichokes 102
5.9 Grilled Veggie Pizza 103
5.10 Portobello Burgers 104
5.11 Easy Grilled Squash 105
5.12 Brown Sugar Grilled Peaches 105
5.13 Warm Artichoke Dip 106
5.14 Grilled Vegetable Platter 108
5.15 Corn with Lemon-Pepper Butter 109
5.16 Smoked Mac and Cheese 109
5.17 Baba Ghanoush 110
5.18 Grilled Shrimp with herbs & Lemon 111
5.19 Bacon-Wrapped Jalapeño Shrimp Poppers 112
5.20 Grilled Bread Salad with Charred Corn and vegetables 113
5.21 Grilled Onion and Sour Cream Dip 114
5.22 Grilled Potatoes 116

Conclusion 117

Introduction

The camp chef, barbecue pit boss or tailgater offer numerous appealing options when it comes to grilling meat. Traditionalists might favor a charcoal smoker or grill, while efficiency freaks might prefer an electric smoker, gas smoker or gas grill. Consider using a wood pellet smoker if you're a fan of outdoor cooking and really want to incorporate several of these methods. A pellet smoker, also defined as a pellet grill, is a wood-burning cooker capable of smoking, grilling, or baking meat. Pellet smokers use food-grade compressed wood pellets, which burn more slowly as well as cleanly at a lower temperature as compared to standard wood chips. Turkey fish, brisket, racks of ribs and more, can all be cooked in a pellet smoker. Pellet smokers also aid in imparting a delectable smoky flavor to the meat. Furthermore, pellet smokers are simple to operate. The meat can be flipped by rotating it in the grilling area, or braising it with a marinade, by simply opening the smoker's lid. Wood pellet grills are available in a variety of models from well-known manufacturers, and they differ in terms of attributes, cooking area, temperature control choices, warming racks, and extras like digital controllers. Almost all are made of stainless steel, but old-school purists may prefer cast-iron models. With so many models available, it's a good idea to consult a buying guide for these devices, especially since new models are added every year. A pellet smoker operates by heating a cooking chamber in which air circulates, heating food through convection. At the lower part of the cooking chamber, charcoal, as well as hardwood pellets, burn, while food is cooked on grill grates near the top. More wood is delivered from a pellet hopper situated above the cooking chamber when the fuel supply runs low. These pellets are pushed down a chute and into the chamber's heart by an auger. Airflow controls the temperature settings on a pellet smoker. Heavy-duty fans close to the bottom of the unit suck air into the lower part of the cooking chamber. From there, the oxygen is consumed by the smoldering pellets. Meanwhile, when the top lid of the smoker is opened, heat can escape. You can cook anything on wood pellet smokers.

- Tri-Tip
- Beef Brisket
- Best Cuts of Meats to Smoke – The Standards

- Beef Chuck Ribs
- Salmon Filet
- Beef Cheeks
- Oysters

And much more

Grill Temperatures

1	Low Heat	250-350 Degrees F
2	Medium Heat	350-450 Degrees F
3	High Heat	450-550 Degrees F

-

CHAPTER 1: Wood Pellet Smoker & Grill Beef Recipes

This chapter contains a number of wood pellet smoker and grill beef recipes that you can select for different occasions.

1.1 Sweet Tea Marinated Ribeyes

Preparation time

8 hours 30 minutes

Servings

4 persons

Ingredients

We have listed below the ingredients that would be required by you for cooking the healthy and tasty meal:

- 1 teaspoon black pepper
- A quarter cup lime juice
- 1 teaspoon salt
- teaspoons sugar
- 1 teaspoon dried minced garlic

- 1 lime thinly sliced
- Sprigs of fresh rosemary
- Rib-eye steaks
- 10 ounces grape or cherry tomatoes halved
- Cups milo's famous sweet tea
- A half tablespoon dried minced onion
- A half tablespoon dried minced garlic
- 1 tablespoon salt
- 10 ounces frozen corn cooked according to package instructions
- 12 ounces crumbled feta
- 15 ounces black beans drained and rinsed
- A quarter cup fresh cilantro chopped

Instructions

Given below are the detailed instructions for cooking this tasty meal. You need to follow these instructions in the given order.

1. Whisk together the onion, salt, tea, garlic and pepper in a large mixing bowl. Insert the lime slices as well as rosemary sprigs in a large zip-lock bag.
2. Put the rib-eyes in the back and seal them properly.
3. Refrigerate the bag for 2-8 hours.
4. Remove the limes, liquid and rosemary from the fridge when ready to cook.
5. Preheat the grill to 400 degrees Fahrenheit.
6. Season each steak with pepper and salt on both sides.
7. Cook for 8-10 minutes per side, or till the internal temperature attains 140-160 degrees Fahrenheit.
8. Serve with Confetti Corn Salad on top.
9. Combine the feta, black bean, tomatoes, corn and cilantro in a large mixing bowl. Whisk together the salt, lime juice, sugar and garlic in a separate small bowl.
10. The sauce mixture is to be poured over the salad and coat it completely with a wooden spoon.

1.2 Porterhouse with Summer Au Poivre Sauce

Preparation time

3 hours 30 minutes

Servings

2-4 persons

Ingredients

We have listed below the ingredients that would be required by you for cooking the healthy and tasty meal:

- ½ cup (packed) mint leaves
- Kosher salt
- 12 lb. porterhouse steak (about 2" thick)
- ½ cup extra-virgin olive oil
- Vegetable oil (for the grill)
- 2 Tbsp. drained pickled green peppercorns
- ½ cup (packed) basil leaves

Instructions

Given below are the detailed instructions for cooking this tasty meal. You need to follow these instructions in the given order.

1. Prepare a grill with high indirect heat.
2. Season the steak with salt and pepper. Grill until deeply browned on all sides at direct heat. You have to keep tenderloin (the smaller side) away from the most intense heat. Remember to keep turning steak every minute or so to control flare-ups as well as ensure even browning.
3. Cook the steak over indirect heat, turning every one to two minutes and moving closer or farther away from the heat as needed to achieve even color, for 10-12 minutes, or unless an instant-read thermometer placed into the thickest part of the steak registers 120° for medium-rare. Allow 15-30 minutes to rest on a wire rack set on a rimmed baking sheet.
4. Cut the meat away from each side of the bone and afterward slice crosswise on a cutting board. Serve with the sauce and the peppercorns that were saved.

1.3 Hasselback Short Rib Bulgogi

Preparation time

3 hours 30 minutes

Servings

4 persons

Ingredients

We have listed below the ingredients that would be required by you for cooking the healthy and tasty meal:

- One tsp. Sugar
- One tablespoon sesame oil toasted
- 1.5-pound 1 inch –1½ inch-thick short ribs, trimmed, boneless beef
- Vegetable oil
- Some Kosher salt
- One tsp. Sesame oil toasted
- 1 tsp. Sesame seeds toasted
- 6 scallions
- Two tsp. Sesame oil toasted
- Two tsp. Rice vinegar unseasoned
- One tsp. Sesame seeds toasted
- One 1" piece of ginger, peeled, grated
- 2 garlic cloves, finely grated
- One scallion, very finely chopped
- ¼ cup white miso
- One tsp. Gochujang (Korean hot pepper paste) or hot chili sauce (such as Sriracha)
- ¼ cup of soy sauce
- Two Tbsp. Rice vinegar unseasoned
- Two Tbsp. Dark or light brown sugar
- One tbsp. Gochugaru

Instructions

Given below are the detailed instructions for cooking this tasty meal. You need to follow these instructions in the given order.

1. In a small bowl, combine the sugar, miso, scallion, gochujang, sesame seeds oil, and one teaspoon water.
2. Scallions should be trimmed and cut in halves lengthwise. Toss the scallions with the vinegar, oil & sesame seeds in a medium mixing bowl.
3. In a medium mixing bowl, combine the vinegar, ginger, garlic, gochugaru, soy sauce, brown sugar & sesame oil.
4. Chop short ribs not more than halfway through the meat with a sharp knife. Turn the scallion over & slice the other side. Toss the meat with the marinade in the bowl, working the marinade into the slashes in the meat. Cover the bowl with a big plate & set it aside for a minimum of two hours or up to a day at room temperature.
5. Prepare the grill for medium heat with the vegetable oil on the grate. Remove the short rib from the marinade and season them lightly with salt. Turn every 1 to 2 mins, and if necessary, move to a chilled area of the grill.
6. Transfer the short rib to the cutting board & set aside for at least five mins before cutting across slashes—or, to be honest, just ripping them apart.
7. Season salt and black pepper over the scallion salad.

1.4 Grilled Steak Tacos

Preparation time

2hours 10 minutes

Servings

4 persons

Ingredients

We have listed below the ingredients that would be required by you for cooking the healthy and tasty meal:

- 1/2 medium tomato, seeded and chopped
- One teaspoon seafood seasoning
- One beef rib-eye steak (1 pound), trimmed
- 8 flour tortillas (6 inches)
- 3 tablespoons sliced ripe olives
- 2 tablespoons canned whole kernel corn
- 2 tablespoons chopped sweet red pepper
- 2 tablespoons lime juice

- 4 teaspoons minced fresh cilantro
- 1/4 cup mayonnaise
- 2 teaspoons Sriracha chili sauce or 1 teaspoon hot pepper sauce
- 1/8 teaspoon sesame oil
- One medium ripe avocado, peeled and finely chopped
- 1 teaspoon kosher salt
- One teaspoon finely chopped onion
- One garlic clove, minced
- 1/4 teaspoon ground cumin
- 2 teaspoons pepper
- 2 teaspoons olive oil
- One teaspoon kosher salt

Instructions

Given below are the detailed instructions for cooking this tasty meal. You need to follow these instructions in the given order.

1. Mix the aioli ingredients in a small bowl. Mix the salsa ingredients in a separate bowl. Refrigerate until ready to serve.
2. Rub both sides of the steak with a mixture of pepper, oil, salt, and seafood seasoning.
3. Cover and cook over medium heat until the meat is done to your liking; for medium-rare, a thermometer must read 135°F. Allow for a 5-minute rest period.
4. In the meantime, warm tortillas on the grill for forty-five seconds on each side
5. Place thinly sliced steak on tortillas. Serve with aioli, salsa, and your favorite toppings.

1.5 Brisket

Preparation time

7 hours

Servings

6 persons

Ingredients

We have listed below the ingredients that would be required by you for cooking the healthy and tasty meal:

- ¼ cup paprika
- 2 tablespoons black pepper
- 2 tablespoons kosher salt
- 5-pound brisket
- ¼ cup brown sugar

Instructions

Given below are the detailed instructions for cooking this tasty meal. You need to follow these instructions in the given order.

1. Remove large chunks of fat as well as the fat cap from the brisket.
2. Choose the rub you want to use.
3. Apply a heavy rub of the spices to all sides of the brisket. It should then be refrigerated for a few hours or overnight after wrapping it in plastic wrap. Remove 1 hour before cooking from the refrigerator and set aside to rest at room temperature.
4. Set up the grill while the brisket is resting. A constant temperature of 225°-250°F is ideal.
5. Then cook on the indirect side.
6. Cook until the internal temperature reaches 200°-205° F.
7. Wrap in foil and a couple of towels after removing them from the grill.
8. Allow it to rest for one to two hours before serving by slicing thinly across the grain.

1.6 Santa Maria Roast Beef

Preparation time

2 hours 30 minutes

Servings

6 persons

Ingredients

We have listed below the ingredients that would be required by you for cooking the healthy and tasty meal:

- 1 tablespoon garlic powder
- 1 beef tri-tip roast or beef sirloin tip roast (2 to 3 pounds)

- 2 cups-soaked hickory wood chips or chunks
- 2 tablespoons canola oil
- 1 tablespoon white pepper
- 1 tablespoon celery salt
- 1 tablespoon ground cumin
- 4 tablespoons paprika
- 3 tablespoons brown sugar
- 2 tablespoons chili powder
- 1 tablespoon dried oregano
- 1 tablespoon pepper
- 2 teaspoons cayenne pepper
- 1 teaspoon ground mustard

Instructions

Given below are the detailed instructions for cooking this tasty meal. You need to follow these instructions in the given order.

1. Combine the ingredients and rub over the roast as desired. Wrap in plastic wrap and place in the refrigerator overnight.
2. 1 hour before grilling, remove the roast from the refrigerator. Using a drip pan, prepare the grill for indirect heat.
3. Unwrap the roast and brush it with oil before placing it over the drip pan. Cover and grill over medium-low indirect heat for one to one and a half hours or until meat reaches desired doneness (a thermometer should read 135 F for medium-rare).

1.7 California Burger Wraps

Preparation time

45 minutes

Servings

8 persons

Ingredients

We have listed below the ingredients that would be required by you for cooking the healthy and tasty meal:

- 8 Bibb lettuce leaves

- 1/2 medium ripe avocado, peeled and cut into 8 slices
- 1/4 cup chopped red onion
- 1/3 cup crumbled feta cheese
- 1-pound lean ground beef (90% lean)
- 1/2 teaspoon salt
- 1/4 teaspoon pepper
- 2 tablespoons Miracle Whip Light

Instructions

Given below are the detailed instructions for cooking this tasty meal. You need to follow these instructions in the given order.

1. Combine beef, salt, and pepper in a large mixing bowl, stirring lightly but thoroughly. Form eight 1/2-inch-thick patties.
2. Then the burgers are to be grilled for three to four minutes on each side at medium heat or broil 3-4 inches from heat till a thermometer reads 160°F. In lettuce leaves, place burgers. Spread feta as well as Miracle Whip on top of burgers.

1.8 Grilled Flank Steak

Preparation time

35 minutes

Servings

4 persons

Ingredients

We have listed below the ingredients that would be required by you for cooking the healthy and tasty meal:

- zest from one lime
- One tablespoon Gourmet Garden Stir-in Chunky Garlic Paste
- 1 tablespoon olive oil
- 2 lbs. Flank Steak
- 1 teaspoon finely chopped green onion
- 1 tablespoon Gourmet Garden Stir-In Chunky Garlic Paste
- 1 teaspoon salt
- 1/2 teaspoon black pepper

- 1/2 cup salted butter softened to room temperature
- One tablespoon Gourmet Garden Lightly Dried Cilantro
- 1 tablespoon fresh lime juice
- 1 teaspoon mustard powder

Instructions

Given below are the detailed instructions for cooking this tasty meal. You need to follow these instructions in the given order.

1. Heat a grill or grill pan over high heat after brushing with canola oil.
2. Combine salt, olive oil, pepper, garlic paste and mustard powder in a small bowl. To make a paste, combine all of the ingredients in a mixing bowl. Apply the paste to both sides of the steak.
3. Grill flank steak for three to four minutes per side for rare, or six to eight minutes per side for well done.
4. Remove the pan from the heat.
5. Cut against the grain into slices.
6. Slice the butter and place it on top of the steak for melting.

1.9 Juicy Grilled Burgers

Preparation time

30 minutes

Servings

4 persons

Ingredients

We have listed below the ingredients that would be required by you for cooking the healthy and tasty meal:

- 4 slices of cheese your favorite
- Avocado slices
- Pineapple slices
- 4 burger buns buttered and toasted
- Mayonnaise
- Ketchup
- Mustard

- 4 ground chuck patties
- Kosher salt
- Freshly ground pepper
- Mayonnaise

Instructions

Given below are the detailed instructions for cooking this tasty meal. You need to follow these instructions in the given order.

1. Using kosher salt as well as freshly ground black pepper, season the four burgers generously.
2. Fill a grill chimney halfway with wood pellets and light it. Preheat the grill for 5 minutes after covering it. After the grate has preheated, clean and oil it.
3. Close the lid and open the vents before placing the burgers directly over the heat. Cook the burgers till the middle of each burger registers 145°F on an instant-read meat thermometer, turning and flipping them frequently.
4. Place the burgers on the grill's cooler side and top with a slice of cheese, if desired. Cook till the cheese is melted as well as the internal temperature reaches 155°F.
5. Cover the burgers with foil and set them aside till ready to eat.

1.10 Jalapeño Popper Burgers

Preparation time

30 minutes

Servings

4 persons

Ingredients

We have listed below the ingredients that would be required by you for cooking the healthy and tasty meal:

- 2 jalapeños, minced
- 1/2 tsp. chili powder
- One and a half Angus ground beef
- Kosher salt
- Freshly ground black pepper
- 4 oz. cream cheese softened
- 1/2 c. shredded cheddar

- 1/2 c. shredded mozzarella
- 6 slices bacon, cooked and chopped
- Four burger buns

Instructions

Given below are the detailed instructions for cooking this tasty meal. You need to follow these instructions in the given order.

1. Make eight large, thin rounds out of ground beef (approximately 14"). Fill one patty with about 14 cups of the filling mixture, then top with a second patty. Pinch the edges of the burger to seal it and, if necessary, reshape it into a disc. Repeat with the rest of the patties as well as a filling mixture.
2. Preheat the grill to medium-high temperature. Salt, chili powder and pepper should be used on both sides of the burgers. Cook till cooked through to your liking on the grill, approximately 6 minutes per side for medium.
3. Serve immediately with burger buns.

1.11 Steak Fajitas

Preparation time

2 hours 40 minutes

Servings

6 persons

Ingredients

We have listed below the ingredients that would be required by you for cooking the healthy and tasty meal:

- A half-cup canola oil
- One large green bell pepper stemmed, seeded and cut into 1/2 -inch-wide strips
- One large yellow or white onions cut
- Twelve pieces of 8-in color or corn tortillas warmed
- 3 tablespoons packed dark brown sugar
- 2 medium cloves garlic minced
- 2 medium jalapeno
- 1 tablespoon fajita seasoning
- 1 teaspoon ground cumin
- A half-cup low-sodium soy sauce

- Half-cup fresh lime juice 5-7 limes
- Juice from 1 large orange
- 1 teaspoon freshly ground black pepper
- Kosher salt to taste
- 2 pounds trimmed skirt steak cut with the grain into 5-inch pieces
- Three medium bell peppers, red, yellow & orange, stemmed, seeded and cut into 1/2 –inch-wide strips

Instructions

Given below are the detailed instructions for cooking this tasty meal. You need to follow these instructions in the given order.

1. Mix fajita seasoning, orange juice, soy sauce, lime juice, jalapenos, canola oil, brown sugar, minced garlic, cumin, and black pepper in a medium mixing bowl.
2. Place the cut steaks in a gallon-sized zip-lock bag with the marinade and seal the bag.
3. Take out the meat from the fridge fifteen to thirty minutes before using it when ready to cook.
4. Insert the cut vegetables into the reserved 12 cup marinade and toss to coat while the meat marinates. Refrigerate, occasionally stirring, until ready to use.
5. Take the meat and vegetables out of the refrigerator.
6. Wipe the surplus marinade from the meat with paper towels.
7. Move the vegetables to the baking sheet with tongs, shaking off any excess marinade as you go.
8. Cook for 4 minutes, then toss to redistribute the vegetables and cook for another 4-5 minutes, or till fork-tender as well as slightly charred.
9. Preheat half of the burners to the highest setting, cover, and wait 10 minutes. Clean as well as oil the grate after 10 minutes.
10. Put the meat on the hot side of the grill, cover, and cook for 6-8 minutes total, occasionally turning, until the steak has a beautiful char on both sides. An instant-read thermometer should read 125-130°F in the center of the meat.
11. Drizzle any remaining meat juices as well as lime juice on top.
12. Serve the meat and vegetables with warmed Mexican rice, salsa, chopped fresh cilantro, sour cream, tortillas, guacamole, Pico de Gallo, beans, cheese and lime wedges on a large serving platter.

1.12 Lacquered Rib Eye

Preparation time

1 hour 20 minutes

Servings

2-4 persons

Ingredients

We have listed below the ingredients that would be required by you for cooking the healthy and tasty meal:

- 2 tsp. sugar
- Flaky sea salt
- Lemon wedges (for serving)
- 1 garlic clove, crushed
- Vegetable oil (for the grill)
- 1 2–2½-lb. bone-in rib eye (about 2" thick),
- ¼ cup sherry vinegar or red wine vinegar
- 2 Tbsp. soy sauce
- 1 Tbsp. fish sauce
- Kosher salt
- Extra-virgin olive oil (for drizzling)

Instructions

Given below are the detailed instructions for cooking this tasty meal. You need to follow these instructions in the given order.

1. In a small saucepan over medium-high heat, bring the sugar, garlic, vinegar, soy sauce and fish sauce to a simmer. Reduce heat to low and gently simmer till the liquid has been reduced by about half.
2. Prepare a grill with a high-intensity indirect heat source.
3. Cook the steak over indirect heat, turning every one to two minutes as well as moving closer to or farther away from the heat as needed to achieve even color, for 10–12 minutes, or till an instant-read thermometer placed in the thickest part of the steak registers 100°F. Begin basting the steak. Grill until the meat is very dark brown, and the thermometer reads 120°F for medium-rare.

4. Slice the steak into thick strips on a cutting board. Arrange on a platter and drizzle with olive oil before seasoning with salt and pepper. Serve with lemon wedges on the side.

1.13 Classic burgers

Preparation time

20 minutes

Servings

3 persons

Ingredients

We have listed below the ingredients that would be required by you for cooking the healthy and tasty meal:

- Three slices of cheese, such as yellow cheddar
- Ketchup
- Mustard
- Mayonnaise
- 3 hamburger buns
- 1 large tomato, thinly sliced
- 1 lb. ground beef
- Kosher salt
- Freshly ground black pepper
- 1 small red onion, thinly sliced
- Three leaves butter or iceberg lettuce

Instructions

Given below are the detailed instructions for cooking this tasty meal. You need to follow these instructions in the given order.

1. Form the beef into three equal-sized patties, each measuring about 3 1/2" in width. Season almost every patty generously with salt and pepper on both sides. Make a shallow indent in the middle of each burger with your finger.

2. Preheat the grill to high heat. Patties should be grilled until a crust forms, and they are no longer pink, about six minutes per side for medium.

3. Before serving, put patties on buns as well as top with desired toppings.

1.14 Pulled Beef Burritos

Preparation time

19 minutes

Servings

4 persons

Ingredients

We have listed below the ingredients that would be required by you for cooking the healthy and tasty meal:

- 1/4 cup light sour cream
- 1/2 cup shredded cheddar cheese
- 1/4 cup BBQ sauce
- 2 tablespoons fresh lime juice
- 1/4 cup fresh cilantro finely chopped
- 2 Large 12-inch flour tortillas
- 1 package Farm Rich Smokehouse Pulled Beef
- 2 cups white rice cooked
- 1 15 ounces can black beans, drained and rinsed

Instructions

Given below are the detailed instructions for cooking this tasty meal. You need to follow these instructions in the given order.

1. Mix the lime juice, cilantro, rice and sour cream in a medium mixing bowl. Stir until everything is well combined and creamy. Remove from the equation.
2. Half of the beef, rice, beans and cheese go into each tortilla. Roll it up like a burrito, bringing the sides in and tucking them in to seal it.
3. Brush the tops of each burrito with a generous amount of BBQ sauce.
4. Grill each burrito for five to seven minutes on each side over medium heat or until the tortilla is crisp and to your liking.
5. Enjoy it with your friends.

1.15 Garlic and Red-Miso Porterhouse

Preparation time

3 hours 30 minutes

Servings

4 persons

Ingredients

We have listed below the ingredients that would be required by you for cooking the healthy and tasty meal:

- 3 tbsp. olive oil
- 8 cloves garlic, grated
- 1 (2") piece ginger, peeled and grated
- 3 tbsp. sesame oil
- 2 (1 1/2"-thick) bone-in porterhouse steaks (3 1/2 lb.)
- 1/2 cup soy sauce
- 1/4 cup red miso
- 1 tsp. freshly ground black pepper

Instructions

Given below are the detailed instructions for cooking this tasty meal. You need to follow these instructions in the given order.

1. In a 9" x 13" baking dish, place the steaks. In a bowl, combine the oil, garlic soy sauce, miso, pepper and ginger; pour 34% of the marinade over the steaks. Set aside for ten minutes after covering with plastic wrap. Save the rest of the marinade.

2. Preheat the grill to high heat. Grill steaks for 1 minute on the hottest part of the grill, without flipping.

3. Move the steaks to the cooler part of the grill and cook for 4 minutes, or until juices appear on top of the steaks. Repeat the grilling process on the other side of the steaks. Return the steaks to the hottest part of the grill and baste with the reserved marinade, flipping and brushing every few minutes until caramelized and the meat starts to shrink away from the bone, ten to twelve minutes for medium-rare.

4. Allow steaks to rest for 5 minutes before slicing against the grain along the bone. Serve and enjoy.

1.16 Top Round Beef Roast Recipe

Preparation time

3 hours 30 minutes

Servings

10 persons

Ingredients

We have listed below the ingredients that would be required by you for cooking the healthy and tasty meal:

- 2 cups beef broth
- One teaspoon garlic salt
- 1/4 cup olive oil
- One tablespoon pepper
- 1 tablespoon barbecue seasoning powder
- 2 1/2 pounds top round beef roast
- 1/4 cup olive oil
- One tablespoon rosemary

Instructions

Given below are the detailed instructions for cooking this tasty meal. You need to follow these instructions in the given order.

1. Rub the mixture all over the meat. Brown the roast on both sides in the oil.
2. Preheat the grill to 400 degrees Fahrenheit.
3. Roast for half an hour, then flip the roast and reduce the heat to 350 degrees Fahrenheit.
4. Cook for an additional 20 minutes, or when the internal temperature attains 130°F.
5. Remove the steak from the grill and set it aside for fifteen minutes before carving.
6. Put the roaster over medium heat just after the roast has been removed.
7. Stir in 2 cups of broth to incorporate the drippings.
8. Cook for 5 minutes on low heat. Pour through a strainer as well as serve with the meat while still warm.

1.17 Brisket Burger

Preparation time

20 minutes

Servings

6 persons

Ingredients

We have listed below the ingredients that would be required by you for cooking the healthy and tasty meal:

- 1 medium yellow onion, sliced 1/4-inch thick
- 2 heirloom tomatoes, cored and sliced 1/4-inch thick
- Ketchup, mayonnaise, and mustard, for serving
- 6 slices cheddar cheese
- 6 burger buns, halved
- 2 lb. beef brisket, ground (ask your butcher to do this)
- Kosher salt and freshly ground black pepper, to taste
- 2 medium red onions, sliced 1/4-inch thick
- Three hearts of romaine halved lengthwise
- Three whole dill pickles, sliced 1/4-inch thick

Instructions

Given below are the detailed instructions for cooking this tasty meal. You need to follow these instructions in the given order.

1. Preheat a gas grill to medium heat.
2. Season meat with pepper and salt and form 6 patties. Place patties in a twelve-inch cast-iron skillet on the grill and top with onion slices. Cover with a grill lid and cook for 3–4 minutes; flip patties and cook for 2 minutes more. Then rest them on top of onion slices.
3. Cook until the cheese is melted, about one to two minutes; keep warm. Grill buns, lettuce, pickles, and tomatoes in batches until charred, about 2 minutes for buns, three to four minutes for romaine, and five to seven minutes for pickles and tomatoes, turning once.

1.18 Boneless Rib Eye with Chimichurri

Preparation time

50 minutes

Servings

2-4 persons

Ingredients

We have listed below the ingredients that would be required by you for cooking the healthy and tasty meal:

- 3/4 cup finely chopped oregano
- Freshly ground black pepper, to taste
- 2 lb. boneless rib eye
- 1 1/2 tsp. crushed red chili flakes
- 1/3 cup olive oil
- 1 tbsp. kosher salt, plus more to taste
- 1 cup finely chopped parsley
- 1/4 cup red wine vinegar
- 8 cloves garlic, finely chopped

Instructions

Given below are the detailed instructions for cooking this tasty meal. You need to follow these instructions in the given order.

1. Preheat a gas grill to high, then turn one burner off.
2. Using paper towels, pat the rib eye dry as well as season liberally with salt and black pepper. Grill for 15-20 minutes on the hottest part of the grill, turning as required, till browned on all sides.
3. Move the rib eye to the cooler side of the grill and cook for another 25-30 minutes for medium-rare, or unless an instant-read thermometer is placed inside the thickest part of the steak registers 125°F.
4. If the outside of the steak starts to burn before it's done, move it to the cooler side of the grill until it's done. Allow 20 minutes for the meat to rest before slicing. Then serve with chimichurri.

1.19 Grilled Cowboy Steak

Preparation time

3 hours 30 minutes

Servings

4 persons

Ingredients

We have listed below the ingredients that would be required by you for cooking the healthy and tasty meal:

- Twelve-pound bone-in rib-eye steak, about 2 1/2 inches thick
- Freshly ground black pepper
- Coarse salt
- Safflower oil or other neutral-tasting oil

Instructions

Given below are the detailed instructions for cooking this tasty meal. You need to follow these instructions in the given order.

1. Allow 1 hour for the steak to rest at room temperature. Using paper towels, pat the steak dry. Preheat the grill to medium-high heat.
2. When the grill is hot, scrub it with a grill brush and lightly oil it. Season both sides of the steak with salt and pepper, then place on the grill with the exposed bone covered in foil to prevent browning. Cover and cook for 5 minutes over direct heat. You also have to rotate the steak 45 degrees halfway through for crosshatch marks; flip and cook for another 5 minutes.
3. Cook for another 6 to 7 minutes per side on indirect heat, flipping once, for medium-rare (125 degrees F on an instant-read thermometer). Remove the steak from the grill and set it aside to rest for ten minutes prior to actually slicing and serving.

1.20 Florentine Steak

Preparation time

3 hours 30 minutes

Servings

4 persons

Ingredients

We have listed below the ingredients that would be required by you for cooking the healthy and tasty meal:

- Two (One and a half-inch thick) bone-in porterhouse steaks (3 1/2 lb.)
- A quarter cup olive oil
- Kosher salt and freshly ground black pepper, to taste
- Two sprigs rosemary
- Lemon wedges, for serving

Instructions

Given below are the detailed instructions for cooking this tasty meal. You need to follow these instructions in the given order.

1. Preheat the wood pellet grill to high and brush half of the oil over the steaks before seasoning with salt and pepper.
2. Grill for 4-6 minutes on the hottest part of the grill, flipping once, till browned. Brush the remaining oil over the steaks with rosemary sprigs.
3. Cook until the desired doneness is reached, about 4-6 minutes longer for medium-rare or unless an instant-read thermometer registers 125°F. If the outside of the steak starts to burn before it's done, move it to the cooler side of the grill till it's done.
4. Allow 5 minutes for the steaks to rest before slicing against the grain along the bone. Serve with lemon wedges on the side.

1.21 Glazed Flank Steak

Preparation time

3 hours 30 minutes

Servings

4-6 persons

Ingredients

We have listed below the ingredients that would be required by you for cooking the healthy and tasty meal:

- A one-third cup of honey
- Orange slices
- Rosemary sprigs
- 1/3 cup fresh orange juice
- 1 tbsp. dark sesame oil
- 1 large clove garlic, crushed and peeled
- Pepper
- 1 cup prepared teriyaki marinade
- A half-cup chopped onion
- One (2-lb.) beef flank steak

Instructions

Given below are the detailed instructions for cooking this tasty meal. You need to follow these instructions in the given order.

1. Lightly score both sides of the flank steak in a crisscross pattern with a sharp knife. Place the steak in the marinade in a dish and turn to coat it. Cover and marinate in the refrigerator for thirty minutes, turning once.
2. Remove the steak from the marinade and discard it. Place the steak on the grill over ash-covered medium coals. For medium-rare to medium, grill uncovered for 17-21 minutes, basting every now and then with reserved marinade as well as turning once.
3. Place the rest of the basting marinade in a small saucepan on the grill grid and bring to a boil. Meanwhile, thinly slice the steak diagonally across the grain and arrange it on a platter. You can, as desired, spoon hot marinade over the beef. Serve with orange slices as well as rosemary sprigs as garnish.

1.22 Angel Cruz Beef Skewers

Preparation time

3 hours 30 minutes

Servings

2-4 persons

Ingredients

We have listed below the ingredients that would be required by you for cooking the healthy and tasty meal:

- 2 shallots, finely chopped
- 1 (1-inch) piece ginger, peeled and minced
- 1 tsp. ground turmeric
- Six tbsp. oyster sauce
- 1 1/2 tbsp. sweet paprika
- 3 lb. beef chuck, cut into 1/2-inch pieces
- Six stalks lemongrass
- 6 kaffir lime leaves, finely chopped
- Six cloves garlic, peeled
- 1/2 cup plus 1 tbsp. honey
- 6 tbsp. vegetable oil
- Six tbsp. fish sauce

Instructions

Given below are the detailed instructions for cooking this tasty meal. You need to follow these instructions in the given order.

1. Combine the lemongrass, turmeric, ginger, lime leaves, garlic and shallots in a food processor and pulse till a smooth paste form. In a large mixing bowl, combine the beef, oyster sauce, honey, fish sauce and paprika. Toss the beef in the sauce until it is evenly coated. Then cover with plastic wrap and chill for at least 3 hours.
2. Preheat the grill. Thread the beef onto wooden skewers and grill, turning as needed, for about 8 minutes, or until charred and cooked through. Transfer to a serving platter and serve immediately.

1.23 Steak Sandwich Kabobs

Preparation time

25 minutes

Servings

4 persons

Ingredients

We have listed below the ingredients that would be required by you for cooking the healthy and tasty meal:

- 6 ounces focaccia bread, cut into 1-inch cubes
- 2 cups deli coleslaw
- 1/2 cup chopped walnuts
- One medium onion, cut into 1-inch chunks
- 1 tablespoon olive oil
- 1 pound beef top sirloin steak, cut into 1-inch cubes
- 1 teaspoon steak seasoning
- One medium sweet red pepper, cut into 1-inch chunks
- 3 slices provolone cheese, cut into strips

Instructions

Given below are the detailed instructions for cooking this tasty meal. You need to follow these instructions in the given order.

1. Steak seasoning should be sprinkled over the beef. Thread the bread cubes, beef, red pepper and onion on 4 metal or soaked wooden skewers in alternate directions; brush with oil.
2. Grill, covered, over medium heat for eight to ten minutes or until desired doneness is reached, turning once or twice. A thermometer must read 135°F for medium-rare, 140°F for medium, and 145°F for medium-well. Grill for an additional 1-2 minutes, or till cheese is melted.
3. Combine the coleslaw and walnuts in a small mixing bowl. Serve alongside kabobs.

1.24 Tacos on a Stick

Preparation time

30 minutes

Servings

4 persons

Ingredients

We have listed below the ingredients that would be required by you for cooking the healthy and tasty meal:

- 2 pounds beef top sirloin steak, cut into 1-inch cubes
- 16 cherry tomatoes
- Salsa con queso or sour cream
- 1 medium green pepper, cut into chunks
- 1 medium sweet red pepper, cut into chunks
- 1 envelope taco seasoning
- 1 cup tomato juice
- 2 tablespoons canola oil
- 1 large onion, cut into wedges

Instructions

Given below are the detailed instructions for cooking this tasty meal. You need to follow these instructions in the given order.

1. Mix the taco seasoning, tomato juice, and oil in a large shallow dish and stir well. Refrigerate the remaining 1/2 cup for basting. Turn the beef to coat it in the sauce. Refrigerate for a minimum of five hours after covering.

2. Remove the beef from the marinade and discard it. Thread beef, peppers, onion, and tomatoes alternately on metal or soaked wooden skewers. Grill for 3 minutes on each side, uncovered, over medium heat. Brush with the marinade that has been set aside. Continue turning and basting till the meat is done to your liking, about 8-10 minutes. Serve with salsa de queso or sour cream, if desired.

1.25 Dry Rubbed Smoked Brisket

Preparation time

11 hours

Servings

12 persons

Ingredients

We have listed below the ingredients that would be required by you for cooking the healthy and tasty meal:

- 6 tbsp chili powder
- 2 tbsp ground coriander
- 2 tsp cayenne pepper
- Raw, unfiltered apple cider vinegar
- 6 tbsp kosher salt
- 4 tbsp cracked black pepper
- 4 tbsp ground cumin
- 12-pound uncured brisket
- 1/2 cup brown sugar
- 1/2 Cup smoked paprika
- 2 tbsp garlic or onion powder
- 2 tbsp dried oregano

Instructions

Given below are the detailed instructions for cooking this tasty meal. You need to follow these instructions in the given order.

1. In a mixing bowl, combine all dry seasonings. Coat the beef on all sides with the dry rub, patting it into the meat. Then the meat is then to be covered with plastic wrap and refrigerated for 15 minutes or up to 4 hours with the fat side up.

2. Heat the smoker to 225 degrees Fahrenheit. Meanwhile, remove the brisket from the refrigerator and set it aside to come to room temperature while remaining cool.

3. Pour half of the apple cider vinegar into the water bowl or pan. Fill the side tray with wood chips.

4. Place the brisket fat side up on the middle rack of the oven. If your smoker has one, place the digital thermometer in the thicker end of the meat. The timer is to be set for ten hours and close the door.

1.26 Beef Suya

Preparation time

45 minutes

Servings

4 persons

Ingredients

We have listed below the ingredients that would be required by you for cooking the healthy and tasty meal:

- 2 teaspoons ground ginger
- One medium onion, cut into wedges
- 1 large tomato, cut into wedges
- Fresh cilantro leaves
- 1 teaspoon crushed red pepper flakes
- 1 teaspoon garlic powder
- 1 beef tri-tip roast or beef top sirloin steak (2 pounds), thinly sliced against the grain
- 1 cup salted peanuts
- 1 tablespoon paprika
- 2 teaspoons onion powder
- Two tablespoons canola oil
- One teaspoon salt

Instructions

Given below are the detailed instructions for cooking this tasty meal. You need to follow these instructions in the given order.

1. Process the peanuts in a food processor until they are finely chopped.
2. Pulse to combine pepper flakes, onion powder, paprika, ginger and garlic powder
3. In a large bowl, place the beef. Drizzle with olive oil and season with salt. Toss to evenly coat. Toss in the peanut mixture and turn to coat. Refrigerate for 2 hours, covered. Drain the beef and toss out the marinade.

4. Using soaked wooden skewers, thread the beef onto the skewers. Cover and grill over medium-high heat for 10-15 minutes or till beef attains desired doneness, turning occasionally. It can be served with onion, tomato, and cilantro before serving.

1.27 Cola Burgers

Preparation time

30 minutes

Servings

4 persons

Ingredients

We have listed below the ingredients that would be required by you for cooking the healthy and tasty meal:

- 1/2 cup saltines, crushed (about 15)
- 1-1/2 pounds ground beef
- 6 hamburger buns, split
- 6 tbsp French dressing of salad, divided
- 2 tbsp Parmesan cheese (grated)
- 1 large egg
- 1/2 cup cola, divided
- 1/4 teaspoon salt

Instructions

Given below are the detailed instructions for cooking this tasty meal. You need to follow these instructions in the given order.

1. Mix a quarter cup cola, egg, cracker crumbs, two tbsp salad dressing, Parmesan cheese & salt in a large mixing bowl. Mix in the beef crumbles thoroughly. Form 6 3/4-inch-thick patties.

2. Set aside the remaining cola as well as a salad dressing in a small bowl.

3. Cover and cook burgers for three minutes on each side over medium heat. Then coat with the cola mixture. Continue grilling for another six to eight minutes, brushing as well as occasionally turning, till the desired doneness is reached. A thermometer must read 135°F for medium-rare.

4. As desired, top burgers with optional toppings

1.28 Grilled Roast Beef Recipe

Preparation time

1 hour

Servings

4 persons

Ingredients

We have listed below the ingredients that would be required by you for cooking the healthy and tasty meal:

- Three-pound beef roast
- cooking oil
- Salt and pepper to taste

Instructions

Given below are the detailed instructions for cooking this tasty meal. You need to follow these instructions in the given order.

1. Turn the grill to high and wait fifteen to twenty minutes for it to heat up.
2. The roast should be rubbed with oil. Season both sides with pepper and salt. If desired, additional seasoning can be added.
3. Place the roast over direct heat when the grill is hot and sear each side for four to five minutes.
4. Let the roast cook for around one hour on the grill for a medium-rare 2-3 pound roast. The grill should be heated to around 400 degrees Fahrenheit. Using a meat thermometer, check for doneness. It should be 145 degrees F for medium-rare.
5. When the roast is about 5 degrees below the desired temperature, remove it from the grill and set it aside for fifteen minutes before carving. As desired, carve and serve.

1.30 Tri-Tip Roast

Preparation time

1 day 60 minutes

Servings

4-6 persons

Ingredients

We have listed below the ingredients that would be required by you for cooking the healthy and tasty meal:

- 2 tsp ground cumin
- Two tsp kosher salt
- A quarter teaspoon kosher salt
- ⅛ teaspoon freshly ground black pepper
- In a small bowl, combine the rub ingredients.
- One teaspoon sweet smoked paprika
- One Roast tri-tip (2-2.5 pounds)
- One tablespoon ground dark-roast coffee
- One tablespoon packed light brown sugar
- One tablespoon ancho chili powder
- One cup sour cream or European-style whole milk yogurt
- 2 tbsp chipotle sauce from the can in adobo
- One clove of garlic pushed through the press or minced
- One tablespoon lime juice (fresh)
- A half tsp ground cumin

Instructions

Given below are the detailed instructions for cooking this tasty meal. You need to follow these instructions in the given order.

1. Whisk together the sauce ingredients in a small bowl. Refrigerate until ready to serve.
2. At medium heat-350° to 450°F- prepare a grill for indirect as well as direct cooking.
3. Sear tri-tip for 10 minutes over medium heat directly with closed lid, turning once. Then grill, covered, over indirect medium-high heat unless a thermometer (instant-

read) placed inside the thicker part of roast records 125°F. Take it out from the grill and set it aside to rest for 10-15 minutes at room temperature indoors.

4. Cut the meat against the grain. Then Serve with adobo sauce on the side.

1.31 Perfectly Grilled Steak

Preparation time

30 minutes

Servings

4 persons

Ingredients

We have listed below the ingredients that would be required by you for cooking the healthy and tasty meal:

- Four one to one and a quarter-inch-thick boneless rib-eye
- Two tbsp canola or extra-virgin olive oil
- Kosher salt and freshly ground pepper

Instructions

Given below are the detailed instructions for cooking this tasty meal. You need to follow these instructions in the given order.

1. Raise the temperature of the grill to high. Brush both sides of the steaks with oil and liberally season with salt and pepper. Place the steaks on the grill and cook for 4 to 5 minutes or till golden brown and slightly charred. Flip the steaks over and cook for another 3-5 minutes for medium-rare (internal temperature of 135°F).

2. Move the steaks to a cutting board and set them aside to rest for 5 minutes before slicing.

CHAPTER 2: Wood Pellet Smoker & Grill Chicken Recipes

This chapter contains a number of wood pellet smoker and grill chicken recipes that you can select for different occasions.

2.1 Chicken Caprese Sandwich

Preparation time

40 minutes

Servings

6 persons

Ingredients

We have listed below the ingredients that would be required by you for cooking the healthy and tasty meal:

- 4 large boneless skinless chicken breasts
- Eight large leaves of fresh basil
- 4 cobblestone hamburger buns
- Salt pepper, and garlic powder to taste

- 4 large slices of tomato
- 2 cups balsamic vinegar
- 3 tablespoons honey
- Eight small slices of fresh whole milk mozzarella

Instructions

Given below are the detailed instructions for cooking this tasty meal. You need to follow these instructions in the given order.

1. Heat up the vinegar as well as honey in a small saucepan over medium/high heat. Bring to a boil. Then reduce to low heat and keep stirring. Remove from the heat and set aside when it begins to thicken and has reduced by almost half.
2. Each breast is to be seasoned with pepper, salt as well as garlic powder to taste. Each breast should be cut lengthwise but not all the way through, forming a pita shape. This is where the basil, mozzarella and tomato will be placed later.
3. Fill two large ziplock bags with the chicken and some of the balsamic reduction, reserving a small amount for garnish. Allow at least thirty minutes in the fridge to marinate before grilling.
4. Spray or brush the cooking grid with nonstick spray or canola oil when you're ready to grill. Stuff one tomato slice, two basil leaves, and two slices of fresh mozzarella into each chicken. If desired, seal the opening with a toothpick to make flipping the chicken easier.
5. Grill the chicken for five to seven minutes on each side over medium/high heat, about 450 degrees F, or until cooked through. The chicken's thickness you choose will determine this. It's done when the chicken is completely white.
6. Drizzle a little bit with the reserved balsamic reduction over the chicken on the bottom bun. Place the top part of the bun on top.

2.2 Grilled Butterflied Chicken with Lemongrass Sauce

Preparation time

4 hours 55 minutes

Servings

4 persons

Ingredients

We have listed below the ingredients that would be required by you for cooking the healthy and tasty meal:

- 2 garlic cloves, finely chopped

- One 3½–4-lb. whole chicken, backbone removed
- 3 Tbsp. vegetable oil
- Purple Sticky Rice
- A half-cup vegetable oil
- A half tsp. Aji-No-Moto umami seasoning
- Kosher salt
- 2 Tbsp. coriander seeds
- 6 scallions, thinly sliced
- 3 lemongrass stalks, bottom third only, tough outer layers removed, finely chopped
- One 2"-piece ginger, peeled, finely chopped
- One Tbsp. cumin seeds

Instructions

Given below are the detailed instructions for cooking this tasty meal. You need to follow these instructions in the given order.

1. In a medium mixing bowl, combine ginger, scallions, lemongrass and garlic. In a small saucepan, heat the oil over high heat until it is hot but not smoking, approximately 2 minutes. Pour the scallion mixture on top. Allow 5 minutes to sit, frequently stirring to avoid burning the aromatics. Season with salt and pepper.

2. In a small dry skillet at medium heat, toast coriander and cumin seeds, frequently shaking, until fragrant as well as slightly darkened in color, approximately 3 minutes. Allow cooling before transferring to a spice mill or mortar and pestle. Transfer spice mixture to a small bowl after finely grinding.

3. Place the chicken on a cutting board, skin side up. Press firmly on the breastbone with your palms to flatten the breast; you could hear a crack. This means you're doing everything correctly. Place the chicken on a large rimmed baking sheet, skin side up. Season both sides generously with salt. Then sprinkle spice mix all over, making sure to get into every nook and cranny. (There may be some spice mix left over.) Underneath the breast, tuck the wings. Chill for a minimum of four hours and up to two days, uncovered.

4. Allow 1 hour for the chicken to come to room temperature before grilling. Drizzle some oil on everything and pat it down.

5. Prepare a grill for indirect medium-high heat-for a gas grill, leave one or two burners off-. Place the chicken on the grate, skin side down, over indirect heat. Place a vent-if your grill has one over the chicken to draw heat up and over it. 15–20 minutes on the grill until the skin is lightly browned. Cook, covered, for another

20-25 minutes, or until the skin is deep golden brown as well as crisp and an instant-read thermometer placed inside the thickest part of the breast registers 160° F. Before carving, transfer the chicken to a cutting board and then let it rest for at least 15 minutes. Serve with rice and lemongrass sauce.

2.3 California Grilled Chicken

Preparation time

40 minutes

Servings

4 persons

Ingredients

We have listed below the ingredients that would be required by you for cooking the healthy and tasty meal:

- Two tbsp. honey
- 4 slices tomato
- 2 tbsp. Freshly sliced basil for garnish
- Balsamic glaze for drizzling
- Two tbsp. extra-virgin olive oil
- 2 tsp. Italian seasoning
- Kosher salt
- Freshly ground black pepper
- 4 boneless skinless chicken breasts
- 3/4 c. balsamic vinegar
- 1 tsp. garlic powder
- Four slices mozzarella
- 4 slices avocado

Instructions

Given below are the detailed instructions for cooking this tasty meal. You need to follow these instructions in the given order.

1. You have to season with pepper and salt. Then whisk together honey, garlic powder, balsamic vinegar, oil and Italian seasoning in a small bowl. Pour over the chicken and set aside for 20 minutes to marinate.

2. Preheat the grill to medium-high when you're ready to cook. Grill chicken till charred as well as cooked through, about 8 minutes per side, on oiled grill grates.

3. Cover the grill for 2 minutes to melt the avocado, mozzarella and tomato on top of the chicken.

4. Drizzle with balsamic glaze and garnish with basil.

2.4 Sticky Grilled Chicken

Preparation time

2 hours 35 minutes

Servings

4 persons

Ingredients

We have listed below the ingredients that would be required by you for cooking the healthy and tasty meal:

- A half-cup low-sodium soy sauce
- A half-cup balsamic vinegar
- 3 tbsp. honey
- 2 cloves garlic, minced
- 2 green onions, thinly sliced
- Two and a half-pound chicken drumsticks
- Vegetable oil for the grill
- Two tbsp. sesame seeds, for garnish

Instructions

Given below are the detailed instructions for cooking this tasty meal. You need to follow these instructions in the given order.

1. Whisk together the garlic, honey, soy sauce, balsamic vinegar and green onions in a large mixing bowl. 1/4 cup marinade should be set aside.

2. Pour the remaining marinade over the chicken in a large re-sealable plastic bag. Allow a minimum of two hours or up to overnight to marinate in the fridge.

3. Preheat the grill to high when you're ready to cook. Grill chicken for 24 to 30 minutes, basting with remaining marinade as well as turning every three to four minutes, till charred and cooked through.

4. Before serving, sprinkle sesame seeds on top.

2.5 Grilled Chicken Breasts with Lemon and Thyme

Preparation time

55 minutes

Servings

4 persons

Ingredients

We have listed below the ingredients that would be required by you for cooking the healthy and tasty meal:

- One and a half tablespoon lemon juice
- One-fourth teaspoon dried thyme
- 1/2 teaspoon dried red-pepper flakes
- 1 clove garlic, minced
- One fourth cup olive oil
- One-fourth teaspoon of salt
- One fourth teaspoon fresh-ground black pepper
- 4 bone-in chicken breasts (about 2 1/4 pounds in all)

Instructions

Given below are the detailed instructions for cooking this tasty meal. You need to follow these instructions in the given order.

1. Turn on the grill. Combine the lemon juice, thyme, black pepper, garlic, red pepper flakes, oil and salt in a shallow dish. Combine the ingredients and coat the chicken.
2. Grill or broil the chicken breasts for 8 to 10 minutes over medium-high heat. Cook for another 10 minutes, or when the chicken is just done.

2.6 Peruvian Chicken

Preparation time

40 minutes

Servings

4-6 persons

Ingredients

We have listed below the ingredients that would be required by you for cooking the healthy and tasty meal:

- 2 tablespoons lime juice
- olive oil for drizzling
- Generous, 5 finger pinches kosher salt
- Squeeze of lime
- Optional bowl additions- cooked cilantro lime rice or mexican pinto beans or both
- Two teaspoons sugar honey or agave
- 1 tbsp cumin
- 2 teaspoons smoked paprika or paprika
- One tsp coriander
- One tsp oregano dried (or one tbsp fresh) or marjoram or sub thyme
- One and a half to two pounds of chicken
- Four garlic cloves- finely minced
- 2 tablespoons olive oil
- One and a half tsp kosher salt
- One tsp soy sauce (it is optional)
- Peruvians green sauce
- A half-cup mayo or sour cream (see the notes for the vegan options)
- Half jalapeño (less if you like less spicy)
- One garlic clove
- One cup cilantro chopped (with thin stems)
- A quarter tsp kosher salt
- Lime squeeze (1 tbsp, save half for the salad)
- Cucumber avocado tomato salad

- Two cups sliced or diced turkish or english cucumber
- 1 big diced avocado, ripe
- A handful of cherry tomatoes (red and yellow ware nice)
- For garnishing, use cilantro leaves

Instructions

Given below are the detailed instructions for cooking this tasty meal. You need to follow these instructions in the given order.

1. Preheat the grill to around medium-high temperature.
2. If you're making rice, get it on the stove right now.
3. In a tiny bowl, make the marinade. Delicately mince garlic as well as place it inside the bowl using a garlic press. Add honey, cumin, paprika, lime juice, oil, honey, coriander, oregano, salt, and soy sauce, if desired. Stir it up a bit. In a mixing bowl, toss them with chicken, coating all the sides well, then brush it on the portobellos. For added flavor, marinate while the grill is heating up or over the night. To make Peruvians Green Sauce, combine all ingredients in the blender & process until smooth, also scraping down sides as needed.
4. When the grill's hot, sear the portobellos and/or chicken on both sides (using the metal spatula for flipping), then reduce the heat or move the chicken to the cooler part of a grill to finish cooking. Because portobellos cook quickly, plate them and cover them with the foil to keep them warm.
5. Place the chopped cucumber in a wide shallow bowl to make the salad. Place the avocado on top, evenly spaced. Add a couple of cherry tomatoes to the mix. Season to taste with salt as well as pepper and a light drizzle of olive oil. Lime juice should be squeezed. Serve with the cilantro leaves as a garnish.
6. Toss with the Lime Cilantro Rice and serve. If making the bowls, start with a three-quarter cup of rice at the bottom of the bowl, followed by sliced portobello or chicken on one side, the avocado salad onto the other, and cilantro sauce drizzled on top.

2.7 Grilled Chicken Shawarma

Preparation time

30 minutes

Servings

6 persons

Ingredients

We have listed below the ingredients that would be required by you for cooking the healthy and tasty meal:

- 8 garlic cloves, minced
- 1 teaspoon ground black pepper
- Two teaspoons allspice
- 2 teaspoons kosher salt
- 6 tablespoons olive oil
- 1/4 teaspoon cayenne pepper
- 2 lbs. to 2 ¼ lb. chicken thighs (boneless and skinless, or skin on- see notes)
- 2 tablespoons ground cumin
- Two tablespoons ground coriander
- Two teaspoon turmeric
- 1 teaspoon ground ginger

Instructions

Given below are the detailed instructions for cooking this tasty meal. You need to follow these instructions in the given order.

1. Combine all of the marinade ingredients in a bowl, as well as stir to combine or pulse to make a paste in a food processor.
2. Marinade the chicken on all sides and set aside for twenty minutes (for a maximum of twenty-four to forty-eight hours refrigerated). You can also skewer the chicken by cutting it into 1-inch cubes.
3. Grill the chicken on a preheated grill over medium-high heat, covered, for about 8 minutes per side, till all sides have nice grill marks. Transfer the chicken to a cooler part of the grill as well as finish cooking it in at 350 F for about 10 minutes, or until fully cooked.
4. Chicken shawarma can be served with Israeli salad, rice and vegetables, or pita bread as well as tzatziki.

2.8 Bratwurst and Chicken Kabobs

Preparation time

50 minutes

Servings

12 kabobs

Ingredients

We have listed below the ingredients that would be required by you for cooking the healthy and tasty meal:

- Two tablespoons stone-ground mustard
- 2 each medium green pepper, sweet red pepper and yellow pepper
- 1 large onion
- 3 tablespoons brown sugar bourbon seasoning
- teaspoon salt
- A half teaspoon of pepper
- 1/2 cup olive oil, divided
- 1 can (15 ounces) peach halves in light syrup, drained and cut into 1/2-in. cubes
- 2/3 cup minced onion
- A quarter cup balsamic vinegar
- 1/4 cup cider vinegar
- Two tablespoons pepper jelly
- 1 jar (12 ounces) mango chutney
- 6 boneless skinless chicken breasts (6 ounces each)
- 1 package (14 ounces) fully cooked bratwurst links

Instructions

Given below are the detailed instructions for cooking this tasty meal. You need to follow these instructions in the given order.

1. Combine the mustard, vinegar, pepper jelly, salt, and pepper in a mixing bowl. Whisk in one-third cup olive oil in a slow, steady stream until well combined. Toss in the peaches, onion, and chutney.
2. Chicken should be cut into 1-inch cubes, and bratwursts should be cut into 1-inch slices. Peppers should be cut into large squares, and onions should be cut into cubes. Toss with the remaining oil and brown sugar bourbon seasoning.

3. Thread meat and vegetables alternately on twelve metal or soaked wooden skewers. Cover and cook skewers on a greased grill rack at medium-high direct heat, turning every now and then, for 10-12 minutes, or till chicken is no longer pink as well as vegetables are tender. During the grilling process, if desired, add more brown sugar bourbon seasoning. Serve with chutney on the side.

2.9 Thai turkey burger

Preparation time

45 minutes

Servings

4 persons

Ingredients

We have listed below the ingredients that would be required by you for cooking the healthy and tasty meal:

- 1 tablespoon lemongrass finely chopped
- A quarter teaspoon of pepper and salt
- A quarter cup mayo, tarter sauce or vegan mayo
- 1-2 tbsp chili garlic or sriracha sauce
- 2 tbsp chopped Thai basil (or reg basil, cilantro, or mint)
- 1 tsp lime zest
- One chopped scallion,
- A half or one jalapeño, finely chopped and seeded,
- 1 tbsp fish sauce (or sub soy sauce)
- One teaspoon sugar
- A quarter teaspoon of white pepper
- 1 lb. Turkey ground
- 3 tbsp shallot, finely diced (or red onion)
- 1.5 teaspoons freshly grated or diced ginger
- 2 cloves of garlic - finely minced (or 1 teaspoon granulated garlic)
- 1 cup of grated carrots
- One cup purple cabbage, shredded
- 1 thinly sliced scallion,

- 2 tbsp wine rice vinegar (or lime juice)
- One tbsp olive oil
- One teaspoon sugar

Instructions

Given below are the detailed instructions for cooking this tasty meal. You need to follow these instructions in the given order.

1. Preheat the grill to medium-high temperature.
2. In a medium mixing bowl, combine all burger ingredients and mix thoroughly with your hands. Form three 1" thick burgers with wet hands. Place in the fridge on a plate.
3. In a medium mixing bowl, combine slaw ingredients.
4. In a small bowl, combine the ingredients for spicy aioli.
5. Grill patties for 4 to 5 mins on every side on a well-greased, preheated grill till golden as well as cooked through.
6. The buns can be toasted or grilled.
7. On bottom bun, spread aioli. Then top with patty, cucumber and slaw.

2.10 Applewood Smoked Chicken

Preparation time

5 hours 15 minutes

Servings

6 persons

Ingredients

We have listed below the ingredients that would be required by you for cooking the healthy and tasty meal:

- One tablespoon smoked paprika
- 1 teaspoon salt
- 1 whole chicken, 4 to 5 pounds
- 1 Tablespoon onion powder
- 1 Tablespoon garlic powder
- ¼ cup dark brown sugar
- 2 Tablespoons chili powder

- One Tablespoon oregano

Instructions

Given below are the detailed instructions for cooking this tasty meal. You need to follow these instructions in the given order.

1. Remove all inside parts of the chicken that need to be discarded, such as the liver, neck, and so on.

2. Place the whole chicken on a cutting board and cut the chicken down the middle of the breast with a meat cleaver. Fill a nine by thirteen glass Pyrex dish halfway with the mixture.

3. Combine all of the dry rub ingredients in a small bowl. Rub the mixture all over the chicken, which is still in the Pyrex dish, until it is gone.

4. Refrigerate the Pyrex dish covered in plastic wrap overnight. The chicken is marinated for a minimum of eight to twelve hours.

5. Turn on your smoker (or light it) after the chicken has marinated and let it preheat until it reaches 225 degrees.

6. Wood chunks or chips should cover the entire wood pan. If you use chunks, you won't have to refill the pan for the duration of the smoke. If you're using wood chips, they'll burn out by the end of the smoke time, so check them every two to three hours and add more if necessary. The smoke pouch aids in the better release of smoke, resulting in more flavor.

7. Put the whole chicken on the rack, breast side up, after the smoker has been preheated and the wood and water pans have been prepared. There will be a lot of smoke for the first two hours. Then it will die down a little. Outside, it will smell wonderful.

8. Smoke the chicken for 4 to 5 hours at 225 degrees Fahrenheit. The temperature in the smoker can occasionally reach 250 degrees F. You'll need to keep an eye on the temperature to make sure the smoker doesn't overheat.

9. Use a digital thermometer at the 4th hour to see how much longer it will take to reach 165 degrees F. Turn the smoker off and take the chicken out when it's done.

10. The internal temperature of the chicken should be 165 degrees.

11. Allow 10 minutes for the chicken to rest before slicing as well as eating.

2.11 Smoked Turkey Breast

Preparation time

4 hours 30 minutes

Servings

8 persons

Ingredients

We have listed below the ingredients that would be required by you for cooking the healthy and tasty meal:

- One 5-7 pounds natural, unbrined whole turkey breast
- ¼ teaspoon crushed red pepper flakes
- One disposable 13×9-inch aluminum foil tray
- 2 cups apple juice or cider or other fruit juice
- 9 tablespoons unsalted butter softened
- Two cloves garlic minced
- 1 teaspoon each fresh diced:
- Oregano leaves
- Thyme leaves
- Rosemary leaves
- 3 quarts cold water
- ½ cup kosher salt
- A quarter cup white sugar
- 2 wood chunks or 2 cups Applewood or Cherry Wood chips
- Sage leaves
- 2 teaspoons Dijon mustard
- 1 teaspoon kosher salt
- A half teaspoon freshly ground black pepper

Instructions

Given below are the detailed instructions for cooking this tasty meal. You need to follow these instructions in the given order.

1. Combine water, salt, and sugar in a large container. Whisk till the salt and sugar are completely dissolved. Place the turkey breast in the water (adding more water if necessary) and refrigerate for 8-12 hours.

2. At least forty-five minutes before cooking, take out the turkey from the fridge and pat it dry.

3. Mix thyme, butter, garlic, sage, oregano, rosemary, mustard, salt, pepper, and red pepper flakes in a small mixing bowl.

4. Cautiously separate the skin from the meat underneath the breast with your fingers.

5. Three tablespoons of herb butter should be applied under the skin of each breast, and the remaining three tablespoons of butter should be applied to the outside of the breasts. To secure the skin to the breast, use 2-3 toothpicks per breast. Toothpicks are used to keep the skin from shrinking during the cooking process.

6. While waiting for the coals to heat, soak the wood chunks in water for up to thirty minutes. If you're using wood chips, soak them first and then pack them in a heavy-duty aluminum foil packet. Make 3-4 slits in the top to allow the smoke to escape.

7. Reduce the heat to medium-low, as well as adjust the burners as needed to maintain an internal temperature of 325°F-350°F on the grill.

8. It's possible that the total cooking time will be one and a half to two and a half hours.

9. The turkey is done when an instant-read thermometer reads 162°F-163°F for the internal temperature. The skin must be beautiful and amber in color.

10. Move the turkey to a cutting board and let it rest for 20-25 minutes before slicing when the internal temperature attains 162°F-163°F level.

11. Serve and have fun.

2.12 Sticky Barbecue Chicken

Preparation time

2 hours 55 minutes

Servings

8-10 persons

Ingredients

We have listed below the ingredients that would be required by you for cooking the healthy and tasty meal:

- Two teaspoon garlic powder
- One tablespoon Dijon mustard
- One tablespoon Louisiana hot sauce

- One tablespoon Worcestershire sauce
- 1.5 teaspoon cayenne pepper
- Twelve bone-in skin-on, chicken thighs
- Juice and Zest of two lemons
- Four tsp. Of Diamond Crystals or 2.5 tsp. Of Morton's kosher salt
- Five Tbsp. Of Barbecue Seasoning, evenly divided
- One tablespoon vegetable oil, and extra for grill
- One small finely chopped onion
- Barbecue Seasoning
- ¼ cup smoked paprika
- 2 tablespoon light brown sugar
- 2 teaspoon chili powder
- 3 finely chopped garlic cloves
- 2 tablespoons sugar, light brown
- ¾ cup of ketchup
- Two tablespoon vinegar, apple cider
- 2 Tbsp. Blackstrap molasses, unsulfured

Instructions

Given below are the detailed instructions for cooking this tasty meal. You need to follow these instructions in the given order.

1. In a small mixing bowl, combine paprika, garlic powder, chili powder, brown sugar, & cayenne.
2. In the large mixing bowl, toss the chicken with the juice & lemon zest to coat. Toss with salt & 4 tablespoons seasoning as well as toss once again to coat evenly. Allow a minimum of two hours and a maximum of twelve hours for chilling.
3. In a medium saucepan, heat 1 tablespoon of oil over medium-high heat. Cook, occasionally stirring, until onion & garlic are tender, about three minutes. Cook, while constantly stirring, for 2 minutes, or until brown sugar gets a little darker. Add the remaining one tablespoon seasoning and cook, constantly stirring, for 30 seconds, or until fragrant. Cook, while constantly stirring, until the ketchup has slightly dark in color, approximately 2 minutes. In a large mixing bowl, combine the vinegar, mustard, molasses, hot sauce & Worcestershire sauce. Bring to boil over the high heat, constantly stirring for 2 minutes. Allow 5 minutes for cooling. Purée in a blender until completely smooth. Set aside the sauce.

4. Prepare the grill for medium indirect heat. Grates should be lightly oiled. 5 minutes over the direct heat, and turning each minute, until chicken is browned on every side. Transfer the chicken to the indirect heat, then cover & grill while turning every five mins or so till the chicken is cooked through. After 18-25 minutes, the thermometer (instant-read) placed inside the thicker part of the thighs has registered 140° to 145° F. Uncover the grill and cook for another 10 minutes, basting with remaining sauce as well as occasionally turning, till the thermometer reads 165° F.

2.13 Grilled Teriyaki Chicken Bowl

Preparation time

4 hours 30 minutes

Servings

4 persons

Ingredients

We have listed below the ingredients that would be required by you for cooking the healthy and tasty meal:

- A quarter cup mirin
- 1-2 avocados (one half, per bowl), peeled, sliced, salted
- 1/3 cup chopped scallions
- 1 tablespoon toasted sesame seeds
- 1-2 teaspoons grated ginger
- 1 cup rice, rinsed well
- 2 cups water
- Cucumber Ribbon Salad
- 1 large English cucumber
- A quarter cup rice wine vinegar
- 1 pound chicken thighs
- 8 ounces shitake mushrooms
- A quarter cup soy sauce
- 1 teaspoon honey or sugar
- A quarter teaspoon of salt
- 1 tablespoon toasted sesame seeds

Instructions

Given below are the detailed instructions for cooking this tasty meal. You need to follow these instructions in the given order.

1. Marinate whole chicken thighs for 4 hours or overnight in a zip-lock bag with soy sauce, mirin and ginger. The longer the cooking time, the more flavor. If desired, shiitake mushrooms could be added to the same bag.

2. Cook the rice after the meat has been marinated and you're ready to grill.

3. In a medium pot, combine the water as well as rinsed rice with a pinch of salt. Bring to a boil, then reduce to low heat and cook for 20 to forty minutes, based on the rice. Cover and set aside till ready to serve.

4. Prep the cucumber salad as well as preheat the grill to medium-high in the meantime.

5. Cucumber should be cut in half lengthwise, and the seeds scraped out with a spoon. Peel long thin strips or "ribbons" onto a couple of paper towels with a vegetable peeler, sharp cheese slicer, or mandolin. Place them in a bowl after blotting with a few more paper towels. Whisk together sugar, rice wine vinegar and salt, and sesame seeds in a small bowl, then pour over cucumber ribbons and toss.

6. Cut the avocado as well as scallions into slices.

7. Grill the chicken as well as shiitake mushrooms over medium-high heat, turning down the heat after the chicken has been marked and cooked through. To avoid burning, shift the shiitakes to a cooler part of the grill or set them aside.

8. Once the chicken is cooked through, slice it and put it in the bowls.

9. Place rice in the center, then grilled chicken on one side, avocado, cucumber salad, and shiitake mushrooms on the other. Add salt to the avocado. Serve with chopsticks and a sprinkle of sesame seeds as well as scallions in the bowl.

2.14 Chicken Breasts with Romesco Sauce

Preparation time

1 hour 57 minutes

Servings

6 persons

Ingredients

We have listed below the ingredients that would be required by you for cooking the healthy and tasty meal:

- One tsp sweet paprika

- One tsp kosher salt
- One tsp smoked paprika
- ¾ teaspoon kosher salt
- A quarter teaspoon of cayenne pepper
- Lemon wedges for serving
- ½ tsp lemon zest finely grated
- ½ tsp dried oregano
- Quarter tsp black pepper freshly ground
- 4 skinless, boneless, chicken breast cut in halves (6-8 ounces each)
- 2 medium bell peppers, red
- A quarter cup extra-virgin olive oil
- A quarter cup fresh lemon juice
- 3 garlic cloves, minced or pushed through a press
- 2 big garlic cloves
- A quarter cup of toasted almonds
- A quarter cup olive oil, extra-virgin
- Two tbsp tomato paste
- Two tbsp sherry vinegar

Instructions

Given below are the detailed instructions for cooking this tasty meal. You need to follow these instructions in the given order.

1. All marinade ingredients should be whisked together in a small bowl.
2. Gently score chicken breasts on smooth side(skin) on the diagonal, making 3-4 very evenly spaced (quarter inch) deep slashes. Place chicken in a mixing bowl. Then pour in marinade, & toss to evenly coat. Cover the chicken with the plastic wrap & chill for a minimum of one hour and a maximum of eight hours, turning it occasionally.
3. Preheat the grill to medium heat- about 400 degrees to 500 degrees F- for direct cooking.
4. Clean cooking grates with a brush. Grill bell pepper over the direct medium heat with lid closed for about twenty mins, turning every five minutes, until blackened all over. Place the peppers in a bowl with plastic wrap over them and steam for ten to fifteen minutes. Take out the peppers from the bowl, peeling away the charred skin and discarding it, as well as the stems. Transfer the peppers to a food

processor after coarsely chopping them. Combine all of the remaining sauce ingredients in a food processor and blend until smooth. Place in a mixing bowl.

5. Preheat the grill to medium heat- about 350 degrees to 450 degrees F- for direct cooking.
6. To avoid flare-ups, remove chicken from the marinade and allow any surplus marinade to drip into a bowl. Remove the marinade and toss it out. Place chicken on an angle to grate bars, smooth (skin) side down, over the direct medium-high heat.
7. Then grill for 4 to 6 minutes on the first side, while the lid is closed, till chicken breasts are very well grilled as well as easily released from grates. Flip chicken and cook for another 4 to 6 minutes, or till the thermometer (instant-read) is placed inside a thicker part of chicken registers at 165 degrees F. The chicken should be removed from the grill and be set aside to rest for 3-5 mins at room temperature indoors. Serve with lemon wedges and romesco sauce.

2.15 Grilled Chicken Burgers

Preparation time

25 minutes

Servings

4 persons

Ingredients

We have listed below the ingredients that would be required by you for cooking the healthy and tasty meal:

- Three tablespoons Worcestershire sauce
- 3 tablespoons olive oil
- 16 hamburger buns, split
- 3 garlic cloves, minced
- A three-quarter cup ranch salad dressing
- 3/4 cup panko bread crumbs
- 3/4 cup grated Parmesan cheese
- 3 teaspoons pepper
- Four pounds ground chicken

Instructions

Given below are the detailed instructions for cooking this tasty meal. You need to follow these instructions in the given order.

1. Combine the first six ingredients in a large mixing bowl. Mix in the chicken lightly but thoroughly. Make sixteen 1/2-inch-thick patties out of the mixture. Brush both sides with oil and chill for 15 minutes, covered, to enable patties to firm up.

2. Grill burgers, covered, at medium heat for 5-6 minutes on each side till a thermometer reads 165°F. Broil 3-4 inches from heat for five to six minutes on each side till a thermometer reads 165°F. Serve with desired toppings on buns.

2.16 Chicken with Salsa Verde

Preparation time

45 minutes

Servings

4 persons

Ingredients

We have listed below the ingredients that would be required by you for cooking the healthy and tasty meal:

- ⅛ Cup lemon juice
- Two tablespoons balsamic vinegar
- salt and pepper to taste
- Scattering of herbs
- 2 tsp lemon zest
- Two tablespoon capers
- One tablespoon caper "juice" from the jar
- 1 anchovy
- ⅓ cup olive oil plus more for cooking
- A quarter teaspoon salt and pepper, or to taste
- 4 to six pieces of bone-in skin-on, chicken – breasts or thighs
- pepper and kosher salt to taste
- One cup of italian parsley (tender stem ok, packed) feels free while sub parting the basil
- Two garlic cloves

- Two lbs. Of heirloom tomatoes
- Two tbsp olive oil

Instructions

Given below are the detailed instructions for cooking this tasty meal. You need to follow these instructions in the given order.

1. Preheat the grill to medium-high to 350°F.
2. Season the chicken on all sides with salt & pepper.
3. Grill chicken on a greased grill at medium heat till grill marks begin to appear on both sides and the grill is completely covered. Place the chicken in a warm oven, not covered, for ten to fifteen minutes, based on the cut of chicken. (Use a thermometer for this.) It should read 160°F for the breasts & 170° F for the thighs. Keep the burgers on a grill inside the cooler spot till they're fully cooked.
4. You should start making Italian Styled Salsa Verdes while the chicken is grilling.
5. In a food processor, combine all of the ingredients and pulse about fifteen times, or till chopped & just combined – however not smooth. Put everything in a bowl & set it aside.
6. Slice the assorted ripped, room temp. Tomatoes & arrange on a platter to make the tomato salad. Drizzle with balsamic vinegar, extra virgin olive oil and season with salt & pepper. For added color, scatter fresh herbs on top.
7. Divide the chicken as well as tomato salad amongst the plates and top with a drizzle of salsa Verde.

2.17 Cuban Mojo Chicken Legs

Preparation time

5 hours 5 minutes

Servings

4 persons

Ingredients

We have listed below the ingredients that would be required by you for cooking the healthy and tasty meal:

- A quarter cup fresh lime juice
- ½ teaspoon freshly ground black pepper
- 4 bone-in whole chicken legs, each
- Lime and orange wedges

- ¼ cup olive oil
- Zest of one orange
- Zest of one lime
- 1 teaspoon ground cumin
- four garlic cloves
- one tiny jalapeño pepper, coarsely chopped and also seeded
- half cup cilantro leaves & tender stems
- A half-cup orange juice (fresh)
- 1 tsp dried oregano
- One and a half tsp kosher salt

Instructions

Given below are the detailed instructions for cooking this tasty meal. You need to follow these instructions in the given order.

1. Mix all marinade ingredients in the bowl of the food processor. Blend in the food processor.
2. Place the chicken in a large re-sealable plastic bag, pour in the marinade, as well as seal the bag. Refrigerate for four to twenty-four hrs., turning bag occasionally to ensure even distribution of the marinade.
3. Over the medium heat (about 350°-450° F), begin preparing the grill for indirect and direct cooking.
4. Remove the chicken from the marinade, reserving the excess liquid in a bag. Fill the small saucepan halfway with the marinade. Bring to boil over medium heat, then reduce to low heat and cook for 2 mins. It should be cooled to room temperature after removing it from the heat.
5. Grill chicken for 40 minutes over the indirect medium-high heat while the lid is closed, then switch to the direct medium-high heat. The skin side must be up. Continue grilling, lid closed, for another 8 to 10 minutes, or till the thermometer (instant-read) placed inside the thicker part of chicken records 165°F as well as chicken is very well marked. Remove it from the grill and set it aside to rest for 3-5 minutes at room temperature indoors.

2.18 Juicy Grilled Chicken Breast

Preparation time

50 minutes

Servings

4 persons

Ingredients

We have listed below the ingredients that would be required by you for cooking the healthy and tasty meal:

- Four cups water
- 1/4 cup Diamond Crystal kosher salt
- 1 1/2 to 2 pounds boneless skinless chicken breasts
- Three tablespoons extra virgin olive oil
- One and a half teaspoon paprika

Instructions

Given below are the detailed instructions for cooking this tasty meal. You need to follow these instructions in the given order.

1. To dissolve the salt in the water, whisk it in a large mixing bowl. In a large mixing bowl, combine the chicken breasts and the brine. Place in the refrigerator for 30 minutes to chill.
2. Prepare your grill so that one side gets a lot of direct heat and the other gets a lot of indirect heat. Alternatively, a grill pan set over medium-high heat can be used.
3. Take the chicken breasts out of the brine and pat them dry. Drizzle with olive oil and evenly sprinkle with paprika.
4. Brush the grill grates with olive oil. Place the chicken breasts on the grill's hot side (or on the grill pan). Allow the chicken to grill, undisturbed, until grill marks appear on the pieces.
5. Turn the chicken pieces over and place them on the cooler side of the grill once they have browned on one side. Allow them to finish cooking while covered.
6. When the chicken's internal temperature attains 155°F, remove it from the grill.
7. Wrap foil around the breasts. While the chicken rests, the residual heat will continue to cook it. Allow five to ten minutes for resting before cutting as well as serving.
8. With pineapple salsa, grilled peppers or just a squeeze of lime, this dish can be delicious.

2.19 Yogurt-Marinated Chicken Thighs

Preparation time

4 hours 15 minutes

Servings

4 persons

Ingredients

We have listed below the ingredients that would be required by you for cooking the healthy and tasty meal:

- One Cup Stonyfield Plain Yogurt
- 1 Tablespoon Olive Oil
- One Tablespoon Garam Masala
- 2 Tablespoons Garlic Paste or 3 Tablespoons minced garlic
- A half Tablespoon Ground Ginger
- 1 teaspoon red pepper flakes
- 1 teaspoon sea salt
- A half teaspoon of black pepper
- Twelve boneless skinless chicken thighs

Instructions

Given below are the detailed instructions for cooking this tasty meal. You need to follow these instructions in the given order.

1. Combine the ingredients and mix well.
2. Toss in the chicken to combine everything. Make sure the chicken is completely covered in yogurt.
3. Refrigerate for 2-4 hours after covering.
4. Oil the grill or the grill pan. Preheat the grill to medium-high heat when ready to cook.
5. Remove the chicken from the yogurt, but don't pat it dry. Cook each chicken thigh for five to six minutes on each side or until the internal temperature reaches 165 degrees Fahrenheit.
6. Serve and have fun.

2.20 Buttermilk Brined Rotisserie Chicken

Preparation time

1 hour 50 minutes

Servings

4-6 persons

Ingredients

We have listed below the ingredients that would be required by you for cooking the healthy and tasty meal:

- 2 tablespoons sugar
- Thyme sprigs, for garnish
- Lemon wedges, for garnish
- 1 tablespoon fresh thyme leaves
- 2 teaspoons finely grated lemon zest
- 1.5-quart buttermilk
- a quarter cup of kosher salt
- six cloves of garlic pushed through the press or minced
- One teaspoon black pepper, freshly ground
- one whole chicken

Instructions

Given below are the detailed instructions for cooking this tasty meal. You need to follow these instructions in the given order.

1. To dissolve the salt and sugar, whisk together all brine ingredients in a bowl big enough to contain the chicken.
2. Refrigerate the chicken, breast side to be down, in the brine for eight to twenty-four hours, turning every now and then.
3. The chicken is to be removed from brine when ready to grill, allowing the excess liquids to be dripping back to the bowl. Remove the brine and discard it. Using paper towels, pat dries the chicken on the inside and out. Secure the legs and wings of chicken with butcher's twine.
4. Using the spit forks, secure trussed chicken onto rotisserie spit.
5. Place the spit on the grill as well as turn on the motor before turning on the grill to ensure that the food fits & spins freely on the rotisserie.

6. Over medium heat (350° to 450°F), prepare grill for the indirect cooking. To catch the drippings from the chicken, put a drip pan on the center of the grill and on the top of the cooking grates.

7. Place spit on the grill, turn on the motor, and position drip pan underneath the chicken.

8. The chicken is to be removed from the spit and remove from the grill. Allow for 5-10 minutes of resting time indoors at room temperature before carving. Cut the trussing into the serving pieces and discard the trussing. Serve along with the lemon wedges and fresh thyme as a garnish.

CHAPTER 3: Wood Pellet Smoker & Grill Lamb Recipes

This chapter contains a number of wood pellet smoker and grill lamb recipes that you can select for different occasions.

3.1 Grilled Herb Crusted Rack of Lamb

Preparation time

30 minutes

Servings

3 persons

Ingredients

We have listed below the ingredients that would be required by you for cooking the healthy and tasty meal:

- 2 teaspoons oregano chopped
- 1/4 teaspoon freshly ground black pepper
- 2 tablespoons olive oil
- 2 teaspoons mint chopped

- 1/2 teaspoon lemon zest
- 1 1/2 - 2-pound rack of lamb trimmed of excess fat
- 3 large cloves garlic minced
- 2 teaspoons rosemary chopped
- 1/2 teaspoon kosher salt

Instructions

Given below are the detailed instructions for cooking this tasty meal. You need to follow these instructions in the given order.

1. To make the marinade, combine all of the ingredients in a small bowl to make a thick paste.
2. Cover the lamb rack with the marinade. Refrigerate for eight hours or overnight, covered in plastic wrap.
3. Preheat the grill to 500°-525° F. Then put the rack of lamb on the grill for 5 minutes to sear the meat.
4. Reduce the temperature to 425°F. Turn the lamb over and roast for another 13-15 minutes, or until the internal temperature of the lamb attains 120° F for medium-rare. Transfer the lamb to a cutting board as well as cover with aluminum foil to keep it warm. Allow the lamb to rest for another 5-10 minutes.
5. Make double-cut chops out of the lamb. Place the lamb on a platter as well as pour meat juices over it. Serve with a sprinkling of fresh herbs on top.

3.2 Steakburger with Tangy Caramelized Onions and Herb Butter

Preparation time

40 minutes

Servings

4 persons

Ingredients

We have listed below the ingredients that would be required by you for cooking the healthy and tasty meal:

- 1/4 teaspoon freshly ground black pepper
- Kosher salt freshly ground black pepper
- 1/4 teaspoon kosher salt

- 1 tablespoon   parsley or tarragon finely chopped
- 1.5 pounds steak, dry-aged (like New York strip or rib-eye; 20 % fat), finely ground
- 4 slices white cheddar cheese
- 4 brioche or other high-quality hamburger buns
- Romaine or green leaf lettuce (for serving)
- 2 tablespoons tomato paste
- 3 tablespoons Worcestershire sauce
- 2 tablespoons white wine vinegar
- 2 tablespoons unsalted butter
- 1 tablespoon light brown sugar
- 2 tablespoons neutral vegetable oil, such as grape seed
- 2 medium onions, thinly sliced
- 1/2 teaspoon kosher salt
- 1/4 cup white wine vinegar
- 2 tablespoons finely chopped shallot (about 1 small shallot)
- 1/2 cup (1 stick) unsalted butter, room temperature
- Neutral vegetable oil, such as grapeseed (for the grill)

Instructions

Given below are the detailed instructions for cooking this tasty meal. You need to follow these instructions in the given order.

1. To make the Tangy Caramelized Onions, combine all of the ingredients in a large mixing bowl.
2. To make the herb butter, combine all of the ingredients in a small mixing bowl.
3. Cut the ground steak into four equal portions. Form into 4"-wide, 3/4-inch-thick patties that are loosely packed. To keep it flat as it grills, make a small indentation in the middle with your thumb.
4. Oil the grates of a grill and heat it to medium-high. Season both sides of the patties with pepper and salt. Grill for 2-3 minutes, indented side down, till lightly charred on the bottom. Give two to three more minutes for medium-rare. Flip, top with cheese as well as continue to grill until the desired doneness is reached.
5. Meanwhile, toast the buns on the grill for about 30 seconds. If using, generously spread Herb Butter on the cut sides of the bun. Close the burgers by layering lettuce, patty, and three tablespoons caramelized onions on the bottom buns.

3.3 Grain Bowls with Grilled Corn, Steak, and Avocado

Preparation time

1 hour 10 minutes

Servings

4 persons

Ingredients

We have listed below the ingredients that would be required by you for cooking the healthy and tasty meal:

- 4 small or 3 large corn ears, shucked
- 2 Tbsp. fresh lime juice
- 1 avocado, peeled, thinly sliced
- Creamy Jalapeño Sauce (for serving)
- two cups whole grains cooked, like quinoa, rice, barley or farro,
- three oz. crumbled Cotija Or feta cheese (about half cup)
- 1 lb. skirt or flank steak
- 1 1/2 tsp. kosher salt, divided, plus more
- 1 tsp. freshly ground black pepper, plus more
- 4 thinly sliced scallions
- 1/4 cup olive oil, extra-virgin

Instructions

Given below are the detailed instructions for cooking this tasty meal. You need to follow these instructions in the given order.

1. Heat a grill pan at medium-high heat. Grill steak unless a thermometer (instant-read) inserted in the middle of the steak records 120 degrees to 125° F for the medium-rare. You should turn the steak occasionally. Move to a cutting board & set it aside to cool for at least ten minutes.
2. Meanwhile, char the corn on all the sides on the grill for about ten minutes. Place on a cutting board & set aside to cool.
3. Corn should be cut off the cobs and placed in a large mixing bowl. Stir in the lime juice, scallions, grains, feta, oil and half teaspoon salt. Divide the corn mixture between the bowls.
4. Against the grain, thinly slice the steak. Serve the steak & avocado on top of the bowls.

5. In the end, season with pepper and salt and drizzle along with jalapeno sauce.

3.4 Racks of Lamb with Roasted-Shallot Vinaigrette

Preparation time

49 minutes

Servings

4 persons

Ingredients

We have listed below the ingredients that would be required by you for cooking the healthy and tasty meal:

- 1 teaspoon Dijon mustard
- 2 tablespoons finely chopped fresh thyme leaves
- ½ teaspoon kosher salt
- ½ teaspoon freshly ground black pepper
- 1 teaspoon finely chopped fresh thyme leaves
- ½ teaspoon kosher salt
- ¼ teaspoon freshly ground black pepper
- 1 large shallot, about 1 ounce, unpeeled
- ¼ cup extra-virgin olive oil, divided
- 1 tablespoon balsamic vinegar
- 2 lamb racks, each 1 to 1½ pounds, frenched
- Extra-virgin olive oil

Instructions

Given below are the detailed instructions for cooking this tasty meal. You need to follow these instructions in the given order.

1. Preheat the grill to medium heat-350° to 450°F- for direct cooking.
2. Brush a small amount of olive oil all over the shallot.
3. Adjust the grill to medium heat-350° to 450°F- for indirect cooking.
4. Brush the lamb with oil, as well as season with thyme, salt, and pepper evenly. To keep the bones from burning, cover them loosely with aluminum foil. Sear the lamb over direct heat, bone side down first, for two to four minutes, turning once, until lightly browned. Place the lamb at indirect medium heat, cover, and cook until done to your liking, about 15 minutes for medium-rare. Remove the chops from

the grill and set them aside to rest for three to five minutes before slicing them into individual chops. With the vinaigrette, serve warm.

3.5 Grilled Lamb Chops

Preparation time

23 minutes

Servings

4 persons

Ingredients

We have listed below the ingredients that would be required by you for cooking the healthy and tasty meal:

- 1 cup olive oil
- 3/4 cup lemon juice
- 1 tablespoon chopped mint
- 1 tablespoon chopped Italian parsley
- 10-12 cloves garlic
- 1 teaspoon salt
- 1/4 teaspoon fresh ground black pepper
- 16 lamb chops
- 2 tablespoons avocado oil
- 2 tablespoons Greek Freak seasoning
- 1/4 teaspoon dry oregano

Instructions

Given below are the detailed instructions for cooking this tasty meal. You need to follow these instructions in the given order.

1. Allow the lamb chops to marinate for 30 minutes in a baggie with one-fourth to one-third cup of the mint sauce.
2. Remove the raw lamb from the marinade, as well as discard the remaining sauce.
3. Heat the pellet grill to 450°F and season your lamb chops with Greek Freak seasoning before placing them on the grill.
4. Cook for three to four minutes per side on each side, then set aside to rest.

3.6 Rosemary Lamb Chops

Preparation time

32 minutes

Servings

4 persons

Ingredients

We have listed below the ingredients that would be required by you for cooking the healthy and tasty meal:

- 1 tbsp rosemary leaves, freshly chopped
- Extra-virgin olive oil
- 2 pounds new potatoes, each about 1½ inches in diameter, quartered
- two teaspoons thyme leaves, freshly chopped
- 3 garlic cloves
- 1 teaspoon kosher salt
- ¾ tsp black pepper, freshly ground
- 8 loin lamb chops, each around 4 ounces & 1¼ inch thick, excess fat to be trimmed

Instructions

Given below are the detailed instructions for cooking this tasty meal. You need to follow these instructions in the given order.

1. Garlic should be roughly chopped. Then salt should be sprinkled on top.
2. Preheat the grill to medium heat (350° to 450°F) for direct cooking.
3. Brush both sides of the lamb chops with oil. Almost half of the seasoning mixture should be applied to both sides of the chops.
4. In a medium mixing bowl, place the cut potatoes. Drizzle 2 tablespoons of oil on top and sprinkle with the remaining portion of the seasoning mix. Toss the potatoes to evenly coat them.
5. Grill the potatoes for fifteen to twenty minutes, turning every five minutes, over direct medium heat with the lid closed. While you're grilling the lamb, remove it from the grill and keep it warm.
6. Grill the lamb chops at direct medium heat with the lid closed, turning once or twice until done to your liking, about 8 minutes for medium-rare. Allow resting for three to five minutes after removing from the grill. With the potatoes, serve warm.

3.7 Fire Roasted Baby Lamb Chops with Smoked Paprika-Orange BBQ Sauce

Preparation time

45 minutes

Servings

4-6 persons

Ingredients

We have listed below the ingredients that would be required by you for cooking the healthy and tasty meal:

- 1 cup fresh orange
- 1 tablespoon clover honey
- 1 tablespoon aged sherry vinegar
- 1 teaspoon finely grated orange zest
- two cups canned pureed plum tomatoes
- half cup ketchup
- one tbsp smoked paprika
- half tsp ground coriander
- two tbsp canola oil, and extra for brushing
- three shallots, chopped
- two cloves garlic, chopped
- 2 tablespoons light brown sugar
- Kosher salt and freshly ground black pepper
- 12 baby lamb chops, bone on

Instructions

Given below are the detailed instructions for cooking this tasty meal. You need to follow these instructions in the given order.

1. For direct grilling, preheat the grill to high. On both sides, brush the lamb with canola oil as well as a season with salt and pepper.
2. Put the chops on the grill for 2 to 3 minutes on each side. Grill for another 2 to 3 minutes after flipping and brushing with some of the sauce. Transfer to a serving platter and top with the reserved sauce.

3.8 Lamb Chops Grilled in Rosemary Smoke

Preparation time

1 hour 17 minutes

Servings

4 persons

Ingredients

We have listed below the ingredients that would be required by you for cooking the healthy and tasty meal:

- 8 garlic cloves, minced
- 8 large rosemary sprigs, stems with leaves (soaked in water at least 30 minutes)
- Rosemary sprig (for garnish)
- 2 teaspoons salt
- 1 teaspoon pepper
- 2 teaspoons olive oil (or more if needed)
- 12 lamb loin chops, trimmed of excess fat (at least 1 1/2 inches/4 cm thick)
- 1/4 cup chopped fresh rosemary leaf (or 2 Tb dried)

Instructions

Given below are the detailed instructions for cooking this tasty meal. You need to follow these instructions in the given order.

1. Prepare the grill for high-heat direct cooking. Place the rosemary stems directly on the charcoal or gas burners. When the rosemary begins to smoke, place the chops over direct heat and cook, covered, for 3-6 minutes on each side, until done to your liking.

2. Insert an instant thermometer away from the bone or cut into the chops near the bone to check for doneness. For medium-rare, take out the chops from the grill when the thermometer reads 130 degrees Fahrenheit (54 degrees Celsius), and the meat is still pink near the bone.

3. Move the chops to a platter and set aside for 5 minutes, covered loosely with aluminum foil.

3.9 Make-Ahead Instant Pot Grilled Ribs

Preparation time

2 hours

Servings

4 persons

Ingredients

We have listed below the ingredients that would be required by you for cooking the healthy and tasty meal:

- 2 tablespoons brown sugar
- two Tbsp. white or red wine vinegar
- two crushed garlic cloves,
- half cup parsley, mint leaves and/or dill, coarsely chopped
- 1 Tbsp. kosher salt
- 1/2 tsp. ground cinnamon
- 4 lb. St. Louis–styles pork spareribs, sliced into 3-4-ribs sections
- quarter cup white wine (dry)
- 1 Tbsp. black peppercorns
- 4 tsp. cumin seeds
- 1 1/2 tsp. crushed flakes of red pepper
- for the grill, use Vegetable oil

Instructions

Given below are the detailed instructions for cooking this tasty meal. You need to follow these instructions in the given order.

1. Preheat the grill to medium-high. Clean and lubricate the grate. Congealed fat should be spooned out of the cooking liquid, and the remaining liquid should be transferred to a small pot. Bring the mixture to boil with vinegar and garlic.
2. Cook occasionally swirling the pan until the liquid has been reduced by 1/2, about three mins. Strain into measuring cup through a fine-mesh sieve.
3. Rub a small amount of oil onto the ribs to coat them lightly. Grill the ribs for about 2 minutes or until they are lightly browned. Turn the ribs over, brush the sauce on the exposed side, & grill for another 2 minutes, or until the underside is slightly browned.

4. Place the ribs on the cutting board and set them aside. Allow 5 to 10 minutes to cool before slicing into the individual ribs. In the end, drizzle the remaining sauce on top, then top with herbs.

3.10 3-Ingredient Grilled Steak, Pineapple, and Avocado Salad

Preparation time

50 minutes

Servings

4-6 persons

Ingredients

We have listed below the ingredients that would be required by you for cooking the healthy and tasty meal:

- One teaspoon freshly ground black pepper, plus more
- 1 pineapple, peeled, cut into 1/2" rounds, center core removed, divided
- 2 pounds New York strip steak (about 3 [1"-thick] steaks)
- One and a half tsp kosher salt, divided, plus more
- 3 tablespoons olive oil, plus more for the grill
- 2 avocados

Instructions

Given below are the detailed instructions for cooking this tasty meal. You need to follow these instructions in the given order.

1. Start by seasoning the steak with one tsp salt and one tsp pepper. Allow it to sit for at least 1 hour at room temperature.
2. In a blender, puree one pineapple round, a half teaspoon salt, and 2 tablespoons water until smooth. Blend in 3 tbsp. Oil till smooth; set aside.
3. Heat a grill to medium-high or a grill pan to medium-high; oil the grill grate or pan. 8–10 minutes for medium-rare, grill steaks as well as leftover pineapple rounds, occasionally turning, till the pineapple is lightly charred as well as an instant-read thermometer inserted in the middle of the steak registers 120°F.
4. Place the steak on a cutting board and set it aside. Allow sitting for at least fifteen minutes before slicing thinly. To keep the pineapple warm, place it on a platter and cover it with foil.
5. Cut avocados in half crosswise around the pit, then use your hands to carefully peel off the skin. Cut each half into 1/2" rings crosswise.

6. Arrange sliced steak, avocado, and pineapple on a platter. Season with salt and pepper and drizzle with pineapple dressing.

CHAPTER 4: Wood Pellet Smoker & Grill Seafood Recipes

This chapter contains a number of wood pellet smoker and grill seafood recipes that you can select for different occasions.

4.1 Grilled Sea Scallops with Corn Salad

Preparation time

1 hour 10 minutes

Servings

6 persons

Ingredients

We have listed below the ingredients that would be required by you for cooking the healthy and tasty meal:

- Salt and freshly ground pepper
- 1/4 cup plus 3 tablespoons safflower oil
- 1 1/2 pounds sea scallops (about 30)
- 1 small shallot, minced

- 2 tablespoons balsamic vinegar
- 2 tablespoons hot water
- 1-pint grape tomatoes halved
- 3 scallions, white and light green parts only, thinly sliced
- 1/3 cup finely shredded basil leaves,
- 1 teaspoon Dijon mustard

Instructions

Given below are the detailed instructions for cooking this tasty meal. You need to follow these instructions in the given order.

1. Cook the corn until tender in a big wok of boiling water (salted), about 5 minutes. Drain and set aside to cool. Remove the kernels from the corn and place them in a large bowl. Season with salt and pepper and add tomatoes, scallions, and basil.

2. Puree the shallot along with the hot water, vinegar and mustard in a blender. Toss the corn salad with the vinaigrette, seasoning it with salt and pepper.

3. Toss the scallops with the remaining one tbsp of oil in a large mixing bowl; season with salt and pepper. A large grill pan should be heated. Add half of the scallops to the pan at a time and cook, turning once, till browned, approximately 4 minutes per batch, over moderately high heat.

4.2 Salmon with Grilled Lemons and Yogurt Sauce

Preparation time

53 minutes

Servings

4 persons

Ingredients

We have listed below the ingredients that would be required by you for cooking the healthy and tasty meal:

- 2 teaspoons fresh dill finely chopped
- ¼ teaspoon lemon zest finely grated
- ¼ tsp Sriracha
- ¼ tsp kosher salt
- one tablespoon olive oil extra-virgin
- ¾ cup Greek-styled yogurt whole milk

- 1 little garlic clove, pushed through the press or minced
- 1 tbsp lemon juice fresh
- 1 tablespoon lemon juice fresh
- one small clove of garlic pushed through the press or minced
- 1 tsp soy sauce
- Freshly ground black pepper
- 1 big lemon, cut (¼-inches) thick, remove seeds
- for garnish, dill sprigs, Fresh
- 1 tsp runny honey
- half teaspoon Sriracha
- four salmon fillets (skin on), each (six to eight ounces) & (1-1¼-inches) thick, bones removed
- some Kosher salt

Instructions

Given below are the detailed instructions for cooking this tasty meal. You need to follow these instructions in the given order.

1. Whisk together sauce ingredients in a small bowl.
2. In a tiny bowl, whisk together marinade ingredients.
3. Brush flesh sides liberally with marinade and season with salt as well as pepper. Allow for 15-30 minutes at room temperature before serving.
4. Place lemon slices onto a plate as well as brush with the leftover marinade on both sides.
5. Preheat the grill to medium heat (about 350°-450°F) for direct cooking. Preheat grill for ten minutes with a griddle and/or big skillet (cast-iron) in the center.
6. Put the salmon on a hot griddle directly with flesh-side downwards first, using a metal spatula to evenly space the fillets, so they're easier to turn. Shut the lid & sear salmon fillets over the direct medium-high heat, covered, for about 3 minutes, or until they can be lifted off griddles without sticking. Toss salmon fillets in the sauce and turn them over. Close lid and cook until the meat is done to your liking, about three to five minutes if you like medium rare, based on thickness.

4.3 Garlic Butter Salmon

Preparation time

25 minutes

Servings

4 persons

Ingredients

We have listed below the ingredients that would be required by you for cooking the healthy and tasty meal:

- 1 tablespoon finely minced fresh rosemary
- 1 teaspoon coarse sea salt
- 1/2 teaspoon pepper
- 4 salmon fillets 6 ounces each
- 1 tablespoon minced garlic about 2 cloves
- 1/2 lemon juiced (about 1 tablespoon)

Instructions

Given below are the detailed instructions for cooking this tasty meal. You need to follow these instructions in the given order.

1. Preheat the grill. Next, liberally spray a grill pan.
2. Mix the rosemary, garlic, lemon juice, salt and pepper in a small bowl or mortar and pestle.
3. Use all of the garlic paste to coat each piece of salmon.
4. Remove the salmon from the refrigerator and spray it four times.
5. Spray the bottom of each piece of salmon and flip it over, so the skin side is up on the grill pan.
6. Cover and cook for 4-5 minutes before flipping each salmon filet.
7. Remove the salmon from the grill when it is fully cooked and serve.

4.4 Lobster Tails with Basil-Lemon Butter

Preparation time

21 minutes

Servings

4 persons

Ingredients

We have listed below the ingredients that would be required by you for cooking the healthy and tasty meal:

- 1 tablespoon fresh lemon juice
- ¼ teaspoon hot pepper sauce
- Butter
- 1¼ cup (2 1/2 sticks) unsalted butter
- 2 tablespoons finely chopped fresh basil leaves
- 1 tablespoon finely grated lemon zest
- A half teaspoon kosher salt
- 4 lobster tails, each 6 to 10 ounces

Instructions

Given below are the detailed instructions for cooking this tasty meal. You need to follow these instructions in the given order.

1. Preheat the grill to medium heat (350° to 450°F) for direct cooking.
2. Melt the butter in a small saucepan at low heat, swirling the pan occasionally. Skim the foam off the top of the melted butter and discard it
3. Heat for at least one minute soon after inserting the butter ingredients
4. Turn off the heat. One-quarter cup of the butter should be reserved for grilling the lobster. To maintain the remaining butter warm for serving, cover the saucepan
5. Brush some of the butter retained for grilling on the meat side of the lobster. Grill the lobster tails, meat side down, for 2 to 3 minutes, depending on size, over direct medium heat with the lid closed. Brush the tops of the shells with a little more butter, turn them over, and grill for another 5 to 8 minutes, or until the meat is white and firm but not dry. Remove the lobster from the grill as well as serve immediately with the reserved butter

4.5 Grilled Cedar Plank Salmon Burgers

Preparation time

30 minutes

Servings

4 persons

Ingredients

We have listed below the ingredients that would be required by you for cooking the healthy and tasty meal:

- 1 half lbs. Salmon Fillets Wild Caught
- One and a half tablespoon Avocado Mayo (you can add mayo of your choice)
- One and a half tbsp. Mustard Stone Ground
- half diced Red Onion,
- 1 diced Celery Stalk,
- 2 tablespoon Fresh Dill
- two minced Garlic Cloves,
- 2 teaspoon Sea Salt
- One teaspoon Black Pepper
- juice of Fresh Lemon,

Instructions

Given below are the detailed instructions for cooking this tasty meal. You need to follow these instructions in the given order.

1. Prior to cooking, soak the cedar plank for a minimum of two hours. Preheat the grill to 350-375 degrees Fahrenheit for the indirect heat.
2. Remove skin as well as the pin bones of salmon before dicing it into little pieces in the food processor. Combine the avocado mayonnaise, salt, stone ground mustard, dill, pepper & garlic in a mixing bowl. Pulse the salmon until it becomes smooth & paste-like.
3. Place salmon mixture in a bowl after removing it from the food processor. Mix in red onion as well as celery until everything is well combined.
4. Form four equal-size patties, two for each plank. Then Grill the salmon for 25 to 30 mins, or until it reaches an internal temp. of 145 degrees Fahrenheit.
5. Serve the burger with the bun and toppings of your choice.

4.6 Grilled Shrimp with Shrimp Butter

Preparation time

30 minutes

Servings

6 persons

Ingredients

We have listed below the ingredients that would be required by you for cooking the recipe.

- 1 tsp Malaysian shrimps paste (only belacan)
- Black pepper
- 24 large shrimp, shelled and deveined
- 1.5 teaspoons lime juice, fresh
- 6 tbsp unsalted butter
- half cup red onion, finely chopped
- 1.5 teaspoon red pepper crushed
- Salt
- 6 big wooden skewers, for thirty minutes, soaked in the water

Instructions

Given below are the detailed instructions for cooking this tasty meal. You need to follow these instructions in the given order.

1. Melt three tablespoons butter in a small skillet. Cook, occasionally stirring, until the onion is softened, about 3 minutes. Cook, constantly stirring, for two minutes, until the red pepper, as well as shrimp paste, are fragrant.

2. Then season with salt and lime juice as well as the remaining three tbsp of butter. Warm the butter with the shrimp.

3. Preheat the grill or grill pan. Salt and pepper the shrimp before threading them on the skewers. Grill for 4 minutes totals over the high heat while turning once, till lightly charred as well as cooked through. Transfer to the serving platter and top with shrimp butter. Serve garnished with mint leaves as well as sprouts.

4.7 Grilled Shellfish and Vegetables al Cartoccio

Preparation time

1 hour 10 minutes

Servings

4 persons

Ingredients

We have listed below the ingredients that would be required by you for cooking the healthy and tasty meal:

- Eight big radishes with few stems attached, cut into halves lengthwise
- 16 littleneck clams, scrubbed
- 24 large mussels, scrubbed
- 4 large basil sprigs
- Four medium tomatoes, cut into halves crosswise
- One red onion, sliced into half-inch-thick wedge through root ends
- For drizzling, use olive oil, extra-virgin
- 1 bunch broccoli
- Eight fat asparagus spears
- Eight small carrots with some stem attached
- Salt
- 16 tiny oysters, like Wellfleet, scrubbed
- Crusty Warm bread, to serve

Instructions

Given below are the detailed instructions for cooking this tasty meal. You need to follow these instructions in the given order.

1. Preheat the grill. Mix all vegetables with olive oil & salt in a large mixing bowl. Remove the broccoli from the oven and grill till lightly charred, approximately one minute each side, over moderately high heat. Place on a large plate.
2. Then drizzle the olive oil over the oysters, mussels and clams, in 4 pairs of foil. Drizzle more olive oil over the vegetables and place them on top of the shellfish. Toss each with a basil sprig, a pinch of salt and one tbsp of water. Fold foil into tidy rectangular packets by folding it tightly.

3. Place the packets on the grill and arrange them as desired. Cover as well as cook at moderate-high heat, while rotating one time or twice, for about 25 minutes, or until packets are sizzling and puffed. Serve immediately with bread.

4.8 Grilled Shrimp with Oregano and Lemon

Preparation time

1hour 30 minutes

Servings

8 persons

Ingredients

We have listed below the ingredients that would be required by you for cooking the healthy and tasty meal:

- 3/4 cup olive oil, extra-virgin
- Freshly ground pepper
- 2 1/2 pounds large shrimp, shelled and deveined
- 1 teaspoon lemon zest, finely grated
- 3 tbsp lemon juice, freshly squeezed
- 1/2 cup of salted capers—washed, soaked for one hour & drained
- half cup of oregano leaves
- one garlic clove, finely minced
- Salt

Instructions

Given below are the detailed instructions for cooking this tasty meal. You need to follow these instructions in the given order.

1. Finely chop drained capers, oregano leaves, & garlic on a cutting board. Shift the mix to a mixing bowl and add a half cup plus two tablespoons olive oil, as well as lemon zest & juice. Season sauce with a pinch of black pepper.

2. Preheat the grill. Toss shrimp with the remaining two tbsp of olive oil in a large mixing bowl and season gently with pepper and salt. Thread shrimps onto the metal skewers as well as grill over the high heat, while turning one time, for 3 minutes per side, or until lightly charred & cooked through. Transfer the shrimp to a platter after removing them from skewers. Serve with a dollop of sauce on the top.

4.9 Grilled Fish

Preparation time

20 minutes

Servings

4 persons

Ingredients

We have listed below the ingredients that would be required by you for cooking the healthy and tasty meal:

- Kosher salt
- Freshly ground black pepper
- 1 tsp. chili powder
- 1 tsp. dried oregano
- 1/4 tsp. cayenne pepper
- 1 1 1/2"-thick fillet skin-on white fish, such as bass or cod
- Lime wedges, for serving

Instructions

Given below are the detailed instructions for cooking this tasty meal. You need to follow these instructions in the given order.

1. Preheat the grill to high heat. Combine chili powder, oregano, cayenne, and salt and pepper in a mixing bowl
2. Season the fish with the spice mixture all over
3. Cook for eight to ten minutes, skin-side down, until almost completely opaque throughout
4. Cook for another 2 to 3 minutes on the other side, or until opaque throughout

4.10 Cajun Garlic Butter Lobster Tails

Preparation time

20 minutes

Servings

4 persons

Ingredients

We have listed below the ingredients that would be required by you for cooking the healthy and tasty meal:

- 1/4 cup butter melted
- 1 tablespoon olive oil
- 3 garlic cloves minced
- 4 lobster tails
- Salt and pepper
- 1 tablespoon cajun seasoning

Instructions

Given below are the detailed instructions for cooking this tasty meal. You need to follow these instructions in the given order.

1. Heat the grill to medium-high. Begin by getting the lobster ready. Butterfly the tail by slicing down the center with kitchen shears. Pull the lobster meat upward by loosening the meat. Season the meat with salt and pepper and place it on a baking sheet.

2. Mix olive oil, melted butter, garlic and Cajun seasoning in a small bowl. Brush on top of the lobster that has been prepared.

3. Place lobster flesh side down on the grill for 3-4 minutes or until lightly charred. Cook for another 5 minutes on the other side, flipping it over and brushing it with the marinade again.

4.11 Lemony Grilled Salmon

Preparation time

30 minutes

Servings

4 persons

Ingredients

We have listed below the ingredients that would be required by you for cooking the healthy and tasty meal:

- Kosher salt
- Freshly ground black pepper
- Two lemons, sliced
- 4 6-oz. skin-on salmon fillets
- Extra-virgin olive oil for brushing

- 2 tbsp. butter

Instructions

Given below are the detailed instructions for cooking this tasty meal. You need to follow these instructions in the given order.

1. Preheat the grill to high heat. Season the salmon with pepper and salt after brushing it with oil. Grill the salmon and lemon slices for 5 minutes per side, or until the salmon is cooked through and the lemons are charred.
2. Top the salmon with a pat of butter and grilled lemons as soon as it comes off the grill. Serve and have fun.

4.12 Grilled Halibut

Preparation time

25 minutes

Servings

4 persons

Ingredients

We have listed below the ingredients that would be required by you for cooking the healthy and tasty meal:

- Freshly ground black pepper
- Kosher salt
- Freshly ground black pepper
- 1 mango, diced
- 1 red pepper, finely chopped
- half diced red onion,
- one minced jalapeno,
- 4 (4-6-oz.) halibut steaks
- 2 tbsp. extra-virgin olive oil
- Kosher salt
- one tbsp. cilantro, freshly chopped
- Juice of one lime

Instructions

Given below are the detailed instructions for cooking this tasty meal. You need to follow these instructions in the given order.

1. Preheat the grill to medium-high, as well as brush both sides of the halibut with oil before seasoning with salt and pepper.
2. Then cook for five minutes per side on the grill until halibut is cooked through.
3. In a medium mixing bowl, combine all ingredients as well as a season with salt and pepper. Serve the salsa alongside the halibut.

4.13 Maple Glazed Salmon Steaks

Preparation time

26 minutes

Servings

4 persons

Ingredients

We have listed below the ingredients that would be required by you for cooking the healthy and tasty meal:

- 1 cup diced grape tomatoes,
- 4 salmon steaks, each about (6 ounces) and (1 inch) thick
- 1½ teaspoon
- ½ teaspoon freshly ground black pepper
- Two thinly sliced scallions, green and white parts
- Two tablespoons parsley leaves chopped (italian)
- 1 tbsp lime juice (fresh)
- ½ tsp ground cumin
- Two ears corn, silk removed and shucked
- olive oil, extra virgin
- One poblano pepper, diced, seeded, about (one cup)
- ½ tsp kosher salt
- A quarter tsp hot sauce
- A quarter teaspoon black pepper, freshly ground
- 2 tbsp maple syrup
- Two tbsp dijon mustard
- One tablespoon olive oil, extra-virgin
- 1 teaspoon lime juice, fresh

- A quarter tsp ground cumin

Instructions

Given below are the detailed instructions for cooking this tasty meal. You need to follow these instructions in the given order.

1. Preheat the grill to medium heat (around 350°-450° F) for direct cooking.
2. Brush corn lightly with oil. With the lid closed, grill the corn at direct medium heat.
3. Put one tablespoon of olive oil, lime juice, hot sauce, mustard, cumin, pepper and salt in a small mixing bowl. Pour the mixture over corn and mix well. While you're preparing the salmon, keep it refrigerated.
4. Preheat the grill to medium heat (about 400°-500° F) for direct cooking.
5. All glaze ingredients should be whisked together in a small bowl.
6. Season both sides of salmon steaks with salt & black pepper. Brush the salmon with the glaze and place it on the grill at direct medium heat. Grill salmon for 8-10 mins, basting one time or twice, with the lid closed, till the steaks can be lifted off cooking grates even without sticking. Cook till a thermometer (instant-read) is placed in the thicker part of salmon records 125°-130° F, then flip the steaks and brush with the glaze.
7. Serve the salmon steaks with the salsa while they're still warm.

CHAPTER 5: Wood Pellet Smoker & Grill Vegetables & Sides Recipes

This chapter contains a number of wood pellet smokers and grill vegetables and side recipes that you can select for different occasions.

5.1 Grilled Eggplant Salad with Freekeh and Yogurt Dressing

Preparation time

50 minutes

Servings

4 persons

Ingredients

We have listed below the ingredients that would be required by you for cooking the healthy and tasty meal:

- A quarter cup Italian parsley, chopped

- 2 tablespoons fresh chopped dill (or mint, or parsley)
- 1-2 garlic cloves finely minced
- 1/4 teaspoon salt, or to taste
- 3 scallions, sliced
- 1 tablespoon lemon zest
- 4 tablespoons olive oil
- 3-4 tablespoons lemon juice
- 1/2 teaspoon salt, more to taste
- 1 cup dry Freekeh
- 2 1/2 cups water
- 1 large eggplant, sliced into 1/4-inch slices
- A quarter cup mint, chopped
- 1/4 cup dill, chopped
- 1/2 teaspoon pepper
- A half teaspoon Aleppo chili flakes
- 1 cup plain thick Greek yogurt
- 1 tablespoon lemon juice

Instructions

Given below are the detailed instructions for cooking this tasty meal. You need to follow these instructions in the given order.

1. Preheat the grill to medium-high temperature.
2. In a medium pot, combine freekeh and water, bring to a boil, cover, and cook for 15-20 minutes, or till water is absorbed as well as freekeh is tender.
3. Brush or spray the eggplant slices with olive oil. You should then season it with salt and pepper. Grill for 3-4 minutes on both sides or till grill marks appear. Then wrap in foil to steam and finish cooking. Toss the eggplant with a fork and cut it into bite-size pieces.
4. In a mixing bowl, combine the cooked freekeh, eggplant, scallions, lemon juice, salt, olive oil, herbs, lemon zest, pepper and spices. Toss everything together. Taste and adjust the salt and lemon as needed. It should have a tangy flavor. As it sits, the smoky flavor will emerge.
5. In a small bowl, whisk together the yogurt sauce ingredients. (If you're making a vegan version, you might need to add a little more lemon)

6. To serve, spread the yogurt dressing on a platter and top with the salad. Serve with torn mint leaves as a garnish.
7. Spread yogurt sauce on the container's bottom for lunch, then spoon salad on top (or keep it separate).
8. Salad will keep in the fridge for 3-4 days with a yogurt dressing on the side.

5.2 Mexican-Style Corn on the Cob

Preparation time

35 minutes

Servings

3 persons

Ingredients

We have listed below the ingredients that would be required by you for cooking the healthy and tasty meal:

- 1 tablespoon fresh lime juice
- ¼ teaspoon chipotle chili powder
- 3 tablespoons grated cotija or Parmigiano-Reggiano® cheese
- 3 tablespoons mayonnaise
- 2 tablespoons sour cream
- ¾ teaspoon prepared chili powder

Instructions

Given below are the detailed instructions for cooking this tasty meal. You need to follow these instructions in the given order.

1. Preheat the grill to medium heat-350° to 450°F- for direct cooking.
2. Mix the spread ingredients in a small bowl and stir well. Mix the topping ingredients in a second small bowl and stir well.
3. Clean the cooking grates with a brush. Grill the corn for 10 to 15 minutes, occasionally turning, over direct medium heat with the lid closed, till the kernels are browned in spots as well as tender. Remove the steaks from the grill.
4. Spread the spread evenly over the corn, then top with the topping. Serve immediately.

5.3 Roasted Root Vegetables with Garlic and Rosemary

Preparation time

40 minutes

Servings

4 persons

Ingredients

We have listed below the ingredients that would be required by you for cooking the healthy and tasty meal:

- 1 medium-sized sweet potato, around 12 ounces, neatly peeled
- 1½ teaspoon kosher salt
- ½ teaspoon freshly ground black pepper
- 3 tbsp olive oil, extra-virgin
- 2 tbsp rosemary leaves, freshly minced
- 1.5 pounds (bulbs only) celery root, trimmed and peeled with a knife
- eight ounces medium-sized carrots, peeled
- eight ounces medium-sized parsnips, peeled
- two tsp minced garlic

Instructions

Given below are the detailed instructions for cooking this tasty meal. You need to follow these instructions in the given order.

1. A big pot of water should be brought to a boil. Cut celery root, parsnips, carrots & sweet potato. Cook for 2 minutes in boiling water with carrots, celery, and parsnips. Add sweet potato & cook for another 6-8 minutes, or when vegetables are somewhat cooked. Drain well & set aside to cool completely.

2. Preheat the perforated grill for about ten minutes and prepare the grill for direct cooking at medium heat-350° to 450°F.

3. Whisk together the pepper, salt, oil, rosemary and garlic in a large mixing bowl. Turn the vegetables in the bowl to coat them.

4. The vegetables are to be spread in a single layer onto grill pan & cooked, turning occasionally, till lightly charred & also quite tender, for about ten minutes over direct medium heat with the lid closed.

5. It should be served warm.

5.4 Spicy Grilled Broccoli

Preparation time

30 minutes

Servings

6 persons

Ingredients

We have listed below the ingredients that would be required by you for cooking the healthy and tasty meal:

- 1 tbsp. low-sodium soy sauce
- 1/4 tsp. crushed red pepper flakes, plus more for serving
- 1/4 c. freshly grated Parmesan
- Lemon wedges, for serving
- 3 tbsp. ketchup
- 1 tbsp. honey
- 3 cloves garlic, minced
- 2 lb. broccoli
- 1/4 c. extra-virgin olive oil
- 2 tbsp. Worcestershire sauce
- 1/2 tsp. kosher salt, plus more for sprinkling
- Freshly ground black pepper

Instructions

Given below are the detailed instructions for cooking this tasty meal. You need to follow these instructions in the given order.

1. Preheat the grill to medium. Trim the fibrous bottom half of the broccoli stem, then cut the broccoli head into quarters to make small trees.
2. Whisk together the oil, Worcestershire sauce, ketchup, soy sauce, honey, and garlic in a large mixing bowl. Use pepper, salt and red pepper flakes to taste. Toss in the broccoli as well as toss to combine. Allow for a 10-minute rest period.
3. Place the broccoli on the grill and season lightly with salt. 8 to 10 minutes on the grill, flipping every two minutes as well as basting with any remaining sauce until broccoli is knife-tender and slightly charred.
4. Serve with lemon wedges, and much more red pepper flakes sprinkled on top.

5.5 Grilled Carrots

Preparation time

25 minutes

Servings

6 persons

Ingredients

We have listed below the ingredients that would be required by you for cooking the healthy and tasty meal:

- 2 tsp. honey
- Kosher salt and pepper
- 2 tbsp. pistachios, toasted and finely chopped
- 1 tsp. harissa paste
- 1/4 c. plain 2% Greek yogurt
- 2 bunches of thin carrots with tops, scrubbed and trimmed
- 1 tbsp. olive oil
- 2 tbsp. tahini
- 2 tbsp. fresh lemon juice

Instructions

Given below are the detailed instructions for cooking this tasty meal. You need to follow these instructions in the given order.

1. Preheat the grill to low. If necessary, cut any large carrots in half lengthwise to make sure that all carrots are the same width. Whisk together the honey, oil and harissa in a large mixing bowl. Toss in the carrots to coat.

2. Place carrots on grill and cook, covered, for 10 to 12 minutes, until charred and tender, rolling or turning carrots halfway through. Place on a serving platter.

3. Meanwhile, combine lemon juice, yogurt, tahini and 1/4 teaspoon salt and pepper in a mixing bowl. Drizzle in two tablespoons warm water gradually, adding more if the mixture becomes too thick. Drizzle the dressing over the carrots and top with pistachios.

5.6 Grilled Pattypans

Preparation time

15 minutes

Servings

2 persons

Ingredients

We have listed below the ingredients that would be required by you for cooking the healthy and tasty meal:

- 2 teaspoons hoisin sauce
- 1/4 teaspoon salt
- 1/8 teaspoon ground ginger
- 1 teaspoon rice vinegar
- 1/2 teaspoon sesame oil
- 6 cups pattypan squash (about 1-1/2 pounds)
- 1/4 cup apricot spreadable fruit

Instructions

Given below are the detailed instructions for cooking this tasty meal. You need to follow these instructions in the given order.

1. Place the squash in a grill basket that has been sprayed with cooking spray. Each side should be grilled for four minutes, covered, over medium heat until tender.
2. Meanwhile, mix the remaining ingredients in a small bowl. Transfer the squash to a serving bowl and toss gently with the sauce.

5.7 Grilled Potato Salad with Chiles and Basil

Preparation time

3 hours 30 minutes

Servings

4 persons

Ingredients

We have listed below the ingredients that would be required by you for cooking the healthy and tasty meal:

- 3 tbsp. fish sauce

- 3 garlic cloves
- 2 cups basil leaves
- 2 tbsp. toasted sesame seeds
- 1 tbsp. honey
- 1/4 cup plus 3 Tbsp. extra-virgin olive oil, plus more for drizzling
- 2 lb. baby Yukon Gold potatoes
- 1/2 cup kosher salt, plus more
- 2/3 cup unseasoned rice vinegar
- 2 red Fresno chilies, thinly sliced
- 1 large red onion

Instructions

Given below are the detailed instructions for cooking this tasty meal. You need to follow these instructions in the given order.

1. In a large saucepan, cover potatoes with three quarts of water. Insert half cup salt. Over medium-high heat, bring to a simmer.

2. Preheat the grill to medium-high heat. In a small bowl, combine the honey, vinegar, fish sauce and three tablespoons of oil. Add the chilies and mix well. Set aside the dressing after seasoning it with salt.

3. Cut the onion in half through the root. Next, cut each half into 5 wedges, keeping the root in place.

4. In a large mixing bowl, finely grate the garlic. 14 cup oil, whisked in. Toss the onion wedges into the mixing bowl. As you add the potatoes to the bowl, lightly smash them with your hands and toss gently to coat them in garlic oil. Next season it with salt and pepper.

5. Cook it for 12–15 minutes on the grill, occasionally turning, until potatoes and onion wedges are charred all over.

6. Toss the potatoes in the dressing to coat them. Combine basil as well as sesame seeds in a bowl.

7. In a serving bowl, place the potato salad. Drizzle some oil on top.

5.8 Grilled Artichokes

Preparation time

43 minutes

Servings

8 persons

Ingredients

We have listed below the ingredients that would be required by you for cooking the healthy and tasty meal:

- 1 tablespoon Kosher salt
- 2 cloves garlic, minced
- Salt & pepper, to taste
- 3 garlic cloves, smashed
- 2 lemon halves
- 3-4 artichokes
- 2-3 quarts of water
- 1/2 cup olive oil

Instructions

Given below are the detailed instructions for cooking this tasty meal. You need to follow these instructions in the given order.

1. Trim the tops and stems off the artichokes before cooking. Remove the fuzzy choke from the middle of each artichoke by slicing it in half and removing it with a spoon. To avoid discoloration, quickly rub with lemon wedges.

2. Fill a large pot halfway with water and set it over medium-high heat to bring to a boil. Squeeze the lemon halves first, then add the garlic cloves, salt and lemon halves to the water. Boil for 15-20 minutes, or until the artichokes are softened as well as fairly tender.

3. Take the artichoke halves out of the water and place them on a baking sheet to dry. Meanwhile, in a mixing bowl, mix olive oil as well as minced garlic. Season each artichoke with salt and pepper after brushing it with garlic as well as olive oil on all sides.

4. Heat the grill to medium-high. Place the artichokes cut-side up on the grill. Grill for three to four minutes, then turn and grill for another 3-4 minutes, cut-side down, until tender and charred. Serve with a dipping sauce of your choice.

5.9 Grilled Veggie Pizza

Preparation time

40 minutes

Servings

4 persons

Ingredients

We have listed below the ingredients that would be required by you for cooking the healthy and tasty meal:

- 1 small sweet red pepper, sliced
- 1 can (8 ounces) pizza sauce
- 2 small tomatoes, chopped
- 2 cups shredded part-skim mozzarella cheese
- 1 small onion, sliced
- 1 tablespoon white wine vinegar
- 1 tablespoon water
- 4 teaspoons olive oil, divided
- 8 small fresh mushrooms, halved
- 1 small zucchini, cut into 1/4-inch slices
- 1 small sweet yellow pepper, sliced
- 2 teaspoons minced fresh basil or 1/2 teaspoon dried basil
- 1/4 teaspoon salt
- A quarter teaspoon of pepper
- 1 prebaked 12-inch thin whole wheat pizza crust

Instructions

Given below are the detailed instructions for cooking this tasty meal. You need to follow these instructions in the given order.

1. Mix the onion, peppers, three tsp oil, mushrooms, zucchini, vinegar, water and seasonings in a large mixing bowl. Place in a grill wok or a grill basket. Cover and cook for 8-10 minutes, or until tender, over medium heat, stirring once.
2. Make sure the grill is set to indirect heat. Brush the remaining oil onto the crust and top with pizza sauce. Grilled vegetables, tomatoes, and cheese go on top. Cover and grill for 10-12 minutes over indirect medium heat, or till edges are

slightly browned as well as cheese is melted. To ensure an evenly browned crust, rotate the pizza halfway through cooking.

5.10 Portobello Burgers

Preparation time

25 minutes

Servings

4 persons

Ingredients

We have listed below the ingredients that would be required by you for cooking the healthy and tasty meal:

- 2 Garlic Cloves minced
- Portobello mushroom
- 4 hamburger buns
- 1/4 cup balsamic vinegar
- 1 Tablespoon soy sauce
- 1 Tablespoon Olive oil
- 1 Tablespoon Melted Butter
- One Tablespoon honey
- Salt and pepper

Instructions

Given below are the detailed instructions for cooking this tasty meal. You need to follow these instructions in the given order.

1. Whisk together the soy sauce, garlic, olive oil, butter, honey, salt, and pepper in a small bowl.
2. Remove the stems from the portobello mushrooms gently to prepare them. Scrape the gills out with a spoon. In a nine by thirteen-inch pan, place the mushrooms. Soak for ten minutes in the marinade.
3. Heat the grill to a medium-high setting. Put the mushrooms on the grilled grill for 5 minutes on each side. Remove the burger from the grill and place it on a bun with your favorite toppings.

5.11 Easy Grilled Squash

Preparation time

20 minutes

Servings

4 persons

Ingredients

We have listed below the ingredients that would be required by you for cooking the healthy and tasty meal:

- Three tablespoons olive oil
- 2 garlic cloves, minced
- 1/4 teaspoon salt
- A quarter teaspoon of pepper
- 1 small butternut squash, peeled and cut lengthwise into 1/2-inch slices

Instructions

Given below are the detailed instructions for cooking this tasty meal. You need to follow these instructions in the given order.

1. Mix the oil, garlic, salt, and pepper in a small bowl. Brush the squash slices with the oil.
2. Cover and grill squash for 4-5 minutes on each side over medium heat until tender.

5.12 Brown Sugar Grilled Peaches

Preparation time

16 minutes

Servings

8 persons

Ingredients

We have listed below the ingredients that would be required by you for cooking the healthy and tasty meal:

- 2 tablespoons brown sugar
- ¼ teaspoon kosher salt
- ⅛ teaspoon ground nutmeg

- ½ teaspoon cinnamon
- 2 large peaches or 4 small
- 2 tablespoons unsalted butter melted
- ¼ teaspoon ground ginger

Instructions

Given below are the detailed instructions for cooking this tasty meal. You need to follow these instructions in the given order.

1. Mix ginger, brown sugar, cinnamon and nutmeg in a small bowl. Remove from the equation.
2. Remove the pit from the peaches and quarter them. Cut small peaches in half to make halves.
3. Brush the cut sides of the peaches with the butter.
4. Preheat the grill (or grill pan) to medium-high heat. Make sure the grill grates are clean and oiled with vegetable oil.
5. Put the peaches cut side down on the hot grill and cook till the grill marks appear about 2 minutes. Grill for two minutes on the other cut side of the peach.
6. Turn the peaches over, as well as sprinkle the brown sugar-spice mixture on top. To help melt the sugar, drizzle the melted butter on top.
7. Cook for 2 minutes, or until the sugar has turned into a glaze as well as the peaches are soft. More brown sugar topping can be added if desired.
8. Transfer the peaches to a serving dish and serve with a scoop of ice cream or a salad.

5.13 Warm Artichoke Dip

Preparation time

29 minutes

Servings

6 persons

Ingredients

We have listed below the ingredients that would be required by you for cooking the healthy and tasty meal:

- 1 cup shredded mozzarella cheese
- Unsalted butter

- ⅓ cup finely grated Parmigiano-Reggiano® cheese
- Grilled baguette slices or crisp flatbread
- 1 can (4 ounces) chopped mild green chili peppers, drained
- ¼ cup sour cream
- 2 teaspoons minced garlic
- 1 can (fourteen ounces) artichoke hearts whole packed in the water, drained & patted dry
- Mayonnaise, ¾ cup
- Six ounces softened cream cheese
- 1 tsp mustard powder
- Quarter tsp hot sauce
- A quarter tsp black pepper, freshly ground

Instructions

Given below are the detailed instructions for cooking this tasty meal. You need to follow these instructions in the given order.

1. Soak wood chips for a minimum of thirty minutes in water.
2. Preheat the grill to medium heat-400 degrees to 450 degrees F- for indirect cooking.
3. Drain as well as add wood chips into the gas grill's smoker box, as directed by the manufacturer, and close the lid. When the smoke starts to appear, grill artichoke hearts at direct heat for 3-5 mins, turning once, until warmed through. Remove the steaks from the grill as well as chop coarsely.
4. Mayonnaise, mozzarella, garlic, chilies, hot sauce, cream cheese, mustard powder, sour cream, and pepper should all be mixed together. Smash cream cheese with the bowl's inside with a wooden spoon to make a paste, then stir until smooth. Add artichoke hearts and mix well.
5. Using butter, lightly coat the inside of an eight-inch skillet (cast-iron). Place artichoke mixture in prepared skillet & sprinkle with Parmigiano-Reggiano ® cheese evenly. Cook for 20 to 25 minutes over the indirect medium heat with lid closed, till browned as well as bubbling on the surface. Serve with slices of grilled baguette as well as crisp flatbread after cooling for 10 minutes.

5.14 Grilled Vegetable Platter

Preparation time

30 minutes

Servings

4 persons

Ingredients

We have listed below the ingredients that would be required by you for cooking the healthy and tasty meal:

- 1 teaspoon dried oregano
- 1 large sweet red pepper, cut into 1-inch strips
- 1 medium yellow summer squash, cut into 1/2-inch slices
- 1 medium red onion, cut into wedges
- 1/2 teaspoon garlic powder
- 1/8 teaspoon pepper
- Dash salt
- 1-pound fresh asparagus, trimmed
- 1/4 cup olive oil
- 2 tablespoons honey
- 4 teaspoons balsamic vinegar
- 3 small carrots, cut in half lengthwise

Instructions

Given below are the detailed instructions for cooking this tasty meal. You need to follow these instructions in the given order.

1. Whisk together the ingredients in a small bowl. In a large mixing bowl, combine 3 tablespoons marinade. Toss in the vegetables and toss to coat. Cover and leave to marinate at room temperature for 1 1/2 hours.
2. Place vegetables on a grilling grid and set them on the grill rack. Cover and grill vegetables over medium heat for 8-12 minutes, occasionally turning, until crisp-tender.
3. On a large serving plate, arrange the vegetables. Drizzle the remaining marinade over the top.

5.15 Corn with Lemon-Pepper Butter

Preparation time

35 minutes

Servings

3 persons

Ingredients

We have listed below the ingredients that would be required by you for cooking the healthy and tasty meal:

- Eight medium ears of sweet corn
- 1 cup butter, softened
- Two tablespoons lemon-pepper seasoning

Instructions

Given below are the detailed instructions for cooking this tasty meal. You need to follow these instructions in the given order.

1. Remove silk by carefully peeling back corn husks within one inch of the bottoms. Replace the husks on the corn and secure them with kitchen string. Fill a stockpot halfway with cold water. Soak for 20 minutes and then drain.

2. Meanwhile, combine butter as well as lemon pepper in a small bowl. Cover and grill corn for 20-25 minutes, or until tender, over medium heat, turning frequently.

3. Remove the string as well as peel back the husks. Corn should be served with the butter mixture.

5.16 Smoked Mac and Cheese

Preparation time

3 hours

Servings

4 persons

Ingredients

We have listed below the ingredients that would be required by you for cooking the healthy and tasty meal:

- ¼ cup butter
- Pepper to taste
- Cooking spray

- 3 cups milk
- 8 oz cream cheese
- 1lb (16 oz) Elbow Macaroni.
- ¼ cup flour
- 24 oz of hand-shredded cheese

Instructions

Given below are the detailed instructions for cooking this tasty meal. You need to follow these instructions in the given order.

1. Put all of the 24 ozs of cheese in a big heat-resistant bowl. Mix in the cheese until it is melted, as well as evenly distributed with the cream sauce.
2. Cook your 1 pound of macaroni in accordance with the package directions if you haven't already. Drain as well as combine with the cheese sauce once done.
3. At this point, you can add whatever sounds good to you. Next, add fresh jalapenos or hot sauce if you want to make it spicier. Next, add bacon and breadcrumbs to give it some crunch. If you want something more savory, garlic and herbs are a good choice.
4. When everything is well combined, spray an eight-by-eight aluminum tray with cooking spray as well as a spoon in your mixture, smoothing it out. Because you don't want to stain a nice pan with smoke, cheap aluminum trays are ideal for recipes like this that you want to throw on the smoker.
5. Put it on the smoker for about 2 hours on indirect heat at 225 degrees F until the top is crisped, but the inside is still nice and gooey.

5.17 Baba Ghanoush

Preparation time

4 hours 5 minutes

Servings

6 persons

Ingredients

We have listed below the ingredients that would be required by you for cooking the healthy and tasty meal:

- ½ lemon, juiced, or more to taste
- ½ pinch cayenne pepper, or to taste
- ½ leaf fresh mint, minced

- 1 tablespoon chopped fresh Italian parsley
- 1 tablespoon and 1 teaspoon and ½ teaspoon tahini, or more to taste
- 1 tablespoon and 1 teaspoon and ½ teaspoon extra-virgin olive oil
- 2 large Italian eggplants
- 1 clove crushed garlic
- 1 teaspoon kosher salt, or to taste
- 1 tablespoon plain Greek yogurt

Instructions

Given below are the detailed instructions for cooking this tasty meal. You need to follow these instructions in the given order.

1. Heat an outdoor grill to medium-high heat and brush the grate lightly with oil. The eggplant's skin is to be pricked with the tip of a knife several times.
2. Place eggplants on the grill directly. While the skin chars, turn it frequently with tongs. Cook for 25 to 30 minutes, or until the eggplants have collapsed and become very soft. Allow cooling in a bowl, covered tightly with aluminum foil, for about 15 minutes.
3. Split the eggplants in half and scrape the flesh into a colander set over a bowl once they've cooled enough to handle. Drain for five to ten minutes.
4. Place the eggplant in a mixing bowl. Mash in the crushed garlic as well as salt until the mixture is creamy but still has some texture, approximately 5 minutes. Combine the olive oil, lemon juice, tahini and cayenne pepper in a mixing bowl. Add the yogurt and mix well.
5. Cover bowl with plastic wrap as well as chill for 3 to 4 hours, or until completely chilled. Then season with salt and pepper to taste. Add the mint and parsley and mix well.

5.18 Grilled Shrimp with herbs & Lemon

Preparation time

1 hour 30 minutes

Servings

8 persons

Ingredients

We have listed below the ingredients that would be required by you for cooking the healthy and tasty meal:

- 1 minced garlic clove,
- Freshly ground pepper
- 2 1/2 pounds large shrimp, shelled and deveined
- Salt
- 3/4 cup extra-virgin olive oil
- 1 teaspoon finely grated lemon zest
- Half cup of salted capers—washed, soaked for one hour & drained
- Half cup of oregano leaves
- 3 tablespoons freshly squeezed lemon juice

Instructions

Given below are the detailed instructions for cooking this tasty meal. You need to follow these instructions in the given order.

1. Thinly slice the drained capers, oregano leaves, and garlic on a cutting board. Transfer the solution to a mixing bowl and add a half cup plus two tbsp olive oil, as well as the lemon zest and juice. Season the sauce with a pinch of black pepper.
2. Preheat the grill. Insert the shrimp with the remaining two tbsp of olive oil in a large mixing bowl and season lightly with salt and black pepper.
3. Thread the shrimp onto metal skewers as well as grill over high heat, turning once, for 3 minutes per side, or until lightly charred and cooked through. Transfer the shrimp to a platter after removing them from the skewers. Serve with a dollop of sauce on top.

5.19 Bacon-Wrapped Jalapeño Shrimp Poppers

Preparation time

23 minutes

Servings

4 persons

Ingredients

We have listed below the ingredients that would be required by you for cooking the healthy and tasty meal:

1. Sixteen big shrimps (21 to 30 count), deveined and peeled, tails to be left on
2. eight slices of bacon, all cut in half crosswise
3. Cheese (Monterey Jack), cut into Sixteen sticks

4. Sixteen pickled pepper jalapeño rings (from a jar)

Instructions

Given below are the detailed instructions for cooking this tasty meal. You need to follow these instructions in the given order.

1. Soak toothpicks for a minimum of thirty minutes in water.
2. Butterfly all shrimps by cutting almost all the way through it from the headend to tail end of its curved back. The tail section should be left alone.

5.20 Grilled Bread Salad with Charred Corn and vegetables

Preparation time

45 minutes

Servings

4-6 persons

Ingredients

We have listed below the ingredients that would be required by you for cooking the healthy and tasty meal:

- 2 tablespoons red wine vinegar
- ½ French or Italian baguette halved lengthwise
- 3 ounces arugula
- 2 cups grape or cherry tomatoes, halved
- 1 tablespoon lemon juice
- 1 tsp kosher salt
- ½ tsp black pepper freshly ground
- 1 small red onion, thinly sliced
- 2 cups (packed) basil leaves
- 1 garlic clove, chopped
- ½ cup extra-virgin olive oil
- 4 ears corn, shucked and silk removed
- Extra-virgin olive oil
- Kosher salt

Instructions

Given below are the detailed instructions for cooking this tasty meal. You need to follow these instructions in the given order.

1. In the food processor's bowl, pulse the basil and garlic until finely chopped. The process to combine the salt, oil, vinegar, lemon juice and pepper. Place in a mixing bowl as well as set aside while you make the salad.

2. Fill a small bowl halfway with cold water and add the onion. Allow for a 15-minute rest period.

3. Preheat the grill to medium heat-350° to 450°F- for the direct cooking.

4. Brush the corn lightly with oil and season with salt. Brush the baguette's cut sides with oil and season lightly with salt.

5. Clean the cooking grates with a brush. Grill the corn for about 10 minutes, occasionally turning, over the direct medium-high heat with lid closed, till slightly charred and softened. Grill the baguette, cut-sides down at first, till grill-marked as well as golden brown during the last three to five minutes of cooking time, turning once.

6. On a cutting board, place the corn and bread. When the ear of corn is cool to handle, lay it flat on the cutting board and slice along the length to remove the kernels with a sharp knife, rotating the ear after each cut till all the kernels are removed. Cut the bread into small pieces.

7. In a medium serving bowl, spread the arugula. Toss the arugula with the tomatoes, corn, and onion, then top with the bread. Combine in a gentle manner. Serve the salad immediately with the vinaigrette drizzled over it.

5.21 Grilled Onion and Sour Cream Dip

Preparation time

30 minutes

Servings

4 persons

Ingredients

We have listed below the ingredients that would be required by you for cooking the healthy and tasty meal:

- ½ Tsp kosher salt
- ¼ teaspoon hot sauce, such as tabasco®
- 2 tablespoons finely chopped fresh chives, divided
- Sturdy potato chips or pita chips
- One cup of sour cream

- ½ cup (4 ounces) softened cream cheese,
- ¼ cup of mayonnaise
- One garlic clove pushed through the press or minced
- 1 tsp kosher salt
- Three medium-sized yellow onions, around 1.5 pounds total
- Two tablespoons olive oil, extra-virgin
- 1 tsp thyme leaves, freshly chopped
- 1 tsp worcestershire sauce
- half teaspoon black pepper, ground

Instructions

Given below are the detailed instructions for cooking this tasty meal. You need to follow these instructions in the given order.

1. Preheat the grill to medium heat-about 350°-450° F- for direct cooking. Clean cooking grates with a brush. After cutting onions in ½ lengthwise, slice them into quarter-inch thick 1/2-moons.
2. Mix the thyme, onions, oil and salt in a large mixing bowl & toss to evenly coat onions.
3. On a large perforated grill pan, spread the onion mixture in an even layer.
4. Arrange grill pan at direct medium-high heat & cook onions, stirring every five minutes, until soft and golden brown, about 25 to 35 minutes.
5. Allow the onions to cool to room temperature after removing the pan from the grill. The onion bits which had turned black should be discarded.
6. Except for the chives, mix all dip ingredients in the food processor. Blend until smooth. Add onions & pulse until the mixture resembles a dip, with remaining onion pieces. Then pulse once with the exception of 12 teaspoon chives. Serve with chips in a bowl with the reserved chives sprinkled on top.

5.22 Grilled Potatoes

Preparation time

25 minutes

Servings

6 persons

Ingredients

We have listed below the ingredients that would be required by you for cooking the healthy and tasty meal:

- 1 tsp. kosher salt
- 1/2 c. extra-virgin olive oil
- 2 tbsp. freshly chopped herbs (such as parsley)
- 1 tsp. freshly ground black pepper
- 4 large Idaho or russet potatoes, cut into wedges
- 2 tsp. garlic powder

Instructions

Given below are the detailed instructions for cooking this tasty meal. You need to follow these instructions in the given order.

1. Bring a pot of salted water to a boil. Next, add the potatoes and cook for 5 to 7 minutes, or until al dente. Drain and set aside to cool.
2. Preheat the grill to medium-high as well as lightly oil the grates. Combine pepper, garlic powder and salt in a large mixing bowl, then stir in olive oil. Toss in the potatoes gently to coat. Remove the potatoes from the oil and set aside any remaining oil in a bowl.
3. Let it remain for 5 minutes on the grill, flipping once, till golden brown.
4. Return the potatoes to the reserved oil mixture and toss them once more.

Conclusion

What are your options if you want to impress your family and friends with a wonderfully smoked piece of meat at your next BBQ party but don't want to go through the trouble of cooking it? In this case, a pellet grill could be ideal. Pellet grills, also known as pellet smokers, work by feeding simple wood pellets into a firebox beneath the grates and regulating the temperature with built-in technology. Some pellet grills come with smartphone apps that allow you to get feeding as well as temperature information right on your phone. Pellet grills have become more popular as a result of this technology, but they are also more expensive. However, just because you're on a budget doesn't mean you can't get one with top-notch features. There are also affordable pellet grills on the market that you can purchase. Pellet grills combine the characteristics of traditional smoke grills with a technologically advanced mechanic to make grilling easier and more productive. All you have to do now is set temperature control & relax while the pellet grill takes care of the rest. The hopper, or storage container, in the pellet grill, is filled with cylindrical food-grade wood pellets. Sawdust is used in these, and it reacts to the high heat and pressure. An auger forces wood pellets inside the chamber according to the temperature and cooking time you set. Pellets in the cooking chamber are automatically ignited by a hot rod. Intake combustion fans fuel the flames so that heat is evenly distributed throughout the cooking chamber, and grill grates are heated to the desired temperature. When you set a 'lower' temperature range on the pellet smoking methods, the mechanism allows for extra smoke to produce. You might have noticed that amount of the smoke produced at the time you first turn on the pellet grill decreases over time. This is due to the fact that as pellet grills & smokers heat up, then they emit less smoke. So, while the food cooked over high heat would undoubtedly be delicious, it won't have a strong smoky flavor. It's important to remember to keep your firepot clean. It takes more time & energy to ignite the pellets or to generate the smoke in a fire pot full of ashes. Enjoy cooking healthy foods with pellet grills.